This Book Belongs To
Shirley Gil

MW00576543

DECODING THE
ENOCHIAN
SECRETS

"By all accounts, Dr. John Dee played a major role in world history, shaping politics, scientific thought, and occultism for centuries. The highly influential 'Enochian' system of magic originated in his 'mystical experiments,' of which he kept meticulous records. Yet the centerpiece of his system has never before been published—an enigmatic book that Dee clearly regarded as a monumental gift from God to humanity, communicated through his angels. John DeSalvo has done a wonderful job putting together all the pieces scattered throughout Dee's manuscripts, including an accessible and systematic introduction. DeSalvo provides valuable suggestions for exploring the book, including meditations and spiritual exercises developed over his many years of investigating Dee's published and unpublished works. Definitely recommended."

JOSEPH PETERSON, AUTHOR OF
JOHN DEE'S FIVE BOOKS OF MYSTERY

DECODING THE ENOCHIAN SECRETS

God's Most Holy Book to Mankind
as Received by
Dr. John Dee from Angelic Messengers

THE ORIGINAL TEXT
WITH COMMENTARY BY

JOHN DeSALVO, Ph.D.

DESTINY BOOKS

Destiny Books
Rochester, Vermont • Toronto, Canada

Destiny Books
One Park Street
Rochester, Vermont 05767
www.DestinyBooks.com

Destiny Books is a division of Inner Traditions International

Library of Congress Cataloging-in-Publication Data

DeSalvo, John A.
  Decoding the Enochian secrets : God's most holy book to mankind as received by Dr.
John Dee from angelic messengers : the original text with commentary / by John DeSalvo.
    p. cm.
  Summary: "The ultimate source text of Enochian Magic never before available in book
form"—Provided by publisher."
  Includes bibliographical references (p.   ) and index.
  ISBN 978-1-59477-364-8 (hardcover)
  1. Enochian magic. 2. Dee, John, 1527-1608. I. Title.
  BF1623.E55D43 2011
  133.4'3—dc22
                                                                        2010035310

Printed and bound in the United States by Lake Book Manufacturing

10 9 8 7 6 5 4 3 2 1

Text design by Priscilla Baker
Text layout by Virginia Scott Bowman
This book was typeset in Garamond Premier Pro with Helios and Gill Sans used as display
typefaces

The artwork in appendix B is reprinted with the permission of the British Library.
Excerpts from Joseph H. Peterson's *John Dee's Five Books of Mystery* (2003) used with
permission.

To send correspondence to the author of this book, mail a first-class letter to the author
c/o Inner Traditions • Bear & Company, One Park Street, Rochester, VT 05767, and we
will forward the communication, or contact the author directly at **drjohn@gizapyramid
.com** or **www.myangelmagic.com**.

*I would like to dedicate
this book to the following people:
My parents, John and Nina DeSalvo;
My wife, Valerie, and my children,
Christopher, Stephen, Paul, and Veronica;
And of course to Dr. John Dee,
who made this all possible.*

CONTENTS

Appendix A

Appendix B
THE COMPLETE BOOK OF ENOCH
(As Given to Dr. Dee by the Angels)

PREFACE

I believe that the publication of this book is one of the greatest undertakings of my life. It may also have a tremendous impact on all of humankind. It is with the greatest humility that I have written this introduction to the most important book ever given to man by the angels. I myself feel that I am but a humble instrument in its writing, and I cannot overemphasize its significance.

According to the angels, the Book of Enoch is the most important document ever given to man by God. It holds all of the secrets of the heavens and the earth, and of the physical and spiritual realms. It was the same book that the prophet Enoch of the Bible was given, which was eventually lost. The angels have restored this book to mankind—the recipient was Dr. John Dee, a sixteenth-century Renaissance mathematician, scientist, scholar, and occultist, who received the book in the form of tables, directly from the angels. Dee was considered the most knowledgeable and intelligent man in England in his day. People from all over Europe and beyond traveled to meet with him and discuss every known topic of interest—the physical sciences, mathematics, navigation, alchemy, magical studies, and beyond. There really was no subject in which Dee was not proficient.

He also had one of the largest libraries in the world, containing one-of-a-kind manuscripts and rare books. He believed that the knowledge and wisdom that he was searching for could not be found in the physical world, but only in the spiritual or higher realms. Thus he began a spiritual quest to try to contact and communicate with angels who could instruct him in the wisdom and knowledge of God. His success began when he met the gifted scryer Edward Kelley (a scryer is one who gazes into a crystal and sees visions clairvoyantly). Together, they made contact with the angels of God, who told them that they would be given the most important book that God had ever given mankind, the lost Book of Enoch. Dr. Dee was to be the second Enoch, in the sense that he brought his own book of Enoch to the world. This is the story of Dr. Dee and this new Book of Enoch.

The book that was given to Dr. Dee by the angels is completely different than what is known to biblical scholars as the apocryphal (and very strange) Book of Enoch. It is claimed that the prophet Enoch, mentioned briefly in Genesis, was the author of that book, which tells of Enoch's travels and experiences through the higher heavens, and also of his contact with angels.

The apocryphal Book of Enoch was an important book for the Hebrews and early Christians, and they used it extensively in their worship. However, it was never accepted into the canon of the current, most commonly used Bible, since the stories it told were so bizarre. Even though it is not part of the common Bible of Protestants and Catholics, much of our theological belief and understanding of angels (known as angelology) comes from it. In fact, the Catholic Church has borrowed heavily from the Book of Enoch in its understanding of the hierarchy and role of angels and the story of their fall.

We will discuss this book and its relationship to the Book of Enoch that Dr. Dee received from the angels. Please keep in mind that they are two completely different books, and even though we will discuss both, our main focus will be on the book that the angels gave to Dr. Dee. We will describe how the angels transmitted this book to him for all of humanity, in the form of tables that he and Kelley recorded. We will read what the angels told Dr. Dee about the importance and significance of this book and, in so doing, we will cover all of the known information currently available to us about the Book of Enoch.

Unfortunately, the angels never interpreted the book for Dr. Dee. The only exception was when, on multiple occasions, Edward Kelley went into a clairvoyant trance and claimed to be able to understand its meaning—but when he came out of the trance, he couldn't remember anything that had been revealed to him.

To date, as far as I know, the book has never been deciphered. Past occultists, like Aleister Crowley, have claimed that they had experienced visions related to the book, but no one has objectively been able to explain the meaning behind its coded structure. After more than four centuries, we are still at the beginning stages of trying to unlock its meaning and potential applicability.

In the hope that someone among us will be able to accomplish this task, I will be teaching you a meditation technique that I believe is very effective in helping you to open up to spiritual vibrations and realms, so that you can explore this book in a spiritual manner. I have personally experienced insights during my meditations on the Book of Enoch; these I will share herein. Perhaps *you* will make some important discovery about this book and its meaning, a discovery that no one else has made.

Inner Traditions/Destiny Books is doing a great service to humanity by publishing this book. It is a large undertaking, and it could not have been done without the permission of the British Library, who preserve the Book of Enoch in their rare manuscript collection and have allowed us to reprint it. Also, what most people don't know is that part of the first leaf of the book is located in a different manuscript collection in the British Library; thus the book was originally incomplete. I have put the entire book together for the first time; you will find it in its entirety in appendix B. As far as I know, this is the last set of known manuscripts of Dr. Dee to see print, making this a truly historic work. (Other diaries and manuscripts of Dee's that have been published in the past are listed in the bibliography for interested readers.)

I am truly honored to be part of this project. Please join me as we begin the journey to discover what we can about the Book of Enoch and its hidden mysteries.

This boke, and holy key, which unlocketh the secrets of God his determination, as concerning the beginning, present being, and ende of the world, is so reverent and holy. . . . So excellent and great are the Mysteries therein contained, above the capacity of man. . . . Out of this, shall be restored the holy bokes, which have perished even from the beginning, and from the first that lived. And herein shall be deciphered perfect truths from imperfect falsehood, True religion from false and damnable errors . . . which we prepare to the use of man.

The angel Uriel to Dr. John Dee regarding
the Book of Enoch, May 5, 1583, from John Dee,
Five Books of Mystery

Thus hath God kept promise with you, and hath delivered you the keys of his storehouses: wherein you shall find (if you enter wisely, humbly, and patiently) Treasures more worth than the frames of the heavens.

The angel Gabriel to Dr. John Dee regarding
the Book of Enoch, July 13, 1584, from Meric
Casaubon, *A True and Faithful Relation*

1

ENOCH OF THE BIBLE

What do you consider to be the most important book in the world? Some would say the Holy Bible, especially if they are Christians or Jews. Muslims would probably say the Qu'ran, Hindus would say the Bhagavad Gita, and others would say whatever holy book their religion claims to be of divine origin. Even the agnostics or atheists would probably pick the Bible or some holy book, since most of our laws and customs originate from these sources, even though they may not believe in their religious teachings. If asked this question, I believe that most people would select a book of allegedly spiritual or divine origin. I think very few would say *Moby Dick* or *Gone with the Wind*.

What this tells you is that the idea of God or spirituality is of foremost importance in people's minds, whether consciously or unconsciously. Deep down, spiritual ideas are the most important aspect of their existence. They want the answers to the big questions: "Who am I?" "Where did I come from?" "What is my purpose here?" "Is there a God?"

What is the greatest mystery in the Bible? I'm sure you've seen documentaries about biblical mysteries. They usually include topics like the miracles of Moses, the lost years of Jesus, Ezekiel's vision of the throne chariot of God, the Ark of the Covenant, Noah's Ark, and interpretations of end-time prophecies. But are these the greatest mysteries of the Bible, or is there something more important and significant that these sources have ignored or are not aware of?

1

The greatest mystery of the Bible, in my opinion, is actually found right in the beginning, in Genesis 5. It contains a long list of the names of the patriarchs, from Adam down to Noah. This list gives only the names of each of the patriarchs, how old they were when they had their first son, the sons' names, and the age of the patriarchs when they died. Here's an example of the first two patriarchs:

> When Adam had lived 130 years, he fathered a son in his own like-
> ness, after his image, and named him Seth. The days of Adam after
> he fathered Seth were 800 years; and he had other sons and daugh-
> ters. Thus all the days that Adam lived were 930 years, and he died.
> When Seth had lived 105 years, he fathered Enosh. Seth lived after
> he fathered Enosh 807 years and had other sons and daughters. Thus
> all the days of Seth were 912 years, and he died.
>
> GENESIS 5:3–8*

This narrative continues through ten patriarchs until we get to Noah—but the careful and observant reader will notice something very different in the list. When we get to the seventh patriarch, whose name is Enoch, he follows a different course than the other nine patriarchs. Enoch does not die, but is taken up by God. Why would something like that have happened to him? Why was he so special? Let's see what the Bible tells us.

> When Enoch had lived 65 years, he fathered Methuselah. Enoch
> walked with God after he fathered Methuselah 300 years and had
> other sons and daughters. Thus all the days of Enoch were 365 years.
> Enoch walked with God, and he was not, for God took him.
>
> GENESIS 5:21–24

---

*Unless otherwise indicated, scripture quotations are from the Holy Bible, English Stan-
dard Version (ESV), copyright 2001 by Crossway Bibles, a publishing ministry of Good
News Publishers, used with permission. All rights reserved.

It seems that God took Enoch because he "walked with God," which is another way of saying he was faithful, loyal, and true to his God. Was he taken and given the privilege of not dying like everyone else because of his obedience and love of God? Many other people in the Bible loved God and were obedient (Noah, Moses, Joseph, Abraham), but they died like everyone else. For some reason, Enoch was special, and God decided to take him. Maybe it wasn't because of what he did, or his faith, but because God had a very special and unique mission for him. If so, what could that mission be? To answer this we need to see if there is other information about Enoch that could give us some insight.

There is a very interesting correlation of these verses with another ancient text that comes from ancient Mesopotamia. The Bible says that Enoch was the seventh descendant of Adam. Also, you must have noticed that these patriarchs lived extremely long lives, but Enoch's life was short in comparison. For example, Adam lived to be 930, Seth lived to be 912, and Jared lived to be 963, but Enoch's life was the shortest by far; he only lived 365 years.

Was this a symbolic age, since it takes 365 days for Earth to revolve around the sun? Was the biblical writer trying to tell us something? It is interesting that the Mesopotamian story of creation also has a list of ten kings (known as the Sumerian Kings List). Each of these kings also lived extremely long lives. In fact, the shortest life span of one of the kings was 10,800 years, and the longest was 64,800 years. It may be significant that their seventh king is named after their sun god, and was also special like Enoch, as we shall see. Did this list of the ten patriarchs, and the story about Enoch in the Bible, as well as the Mesopotamian list of the Sumerian kings, and their seventh king, come from a much older common source that they both used to create their own versions? Or did our biblical writers or editors borrow from this older Mesopotamian story to create the genealogies and story of Enoch in Genesis? For some reason, both the Mesopotamian and biblical writers felt that what happened to Enoch or their seventh king was important, and should be included in their most sacred writings.

I'd like to go into more detail regarding this interesting and important historical parallel between the Sumerian Kings List and the biblical list of the patriarchs in Genesis. The seventh Sumerian king is called Enmeduranki, who is associated with the city of Sippar, home of a sun god cult. Sumerian legend has it that this god was initiated into the mysteries of the earth and heavens, just like Enoch, as we shall see in chapter 3 when discussing his travels through the heavens. This is an extremely interesting parallel, and the question still remains—was a common source used for both of these lists, or did one borrow from the other? Either way, both Enoch and his Sumerian counterpart are associated with the mysteries of heaven and earth. This may also imply that the biblical phrase in Genesis that Enoch walked with God may not mean a divine fellowship, but an initiation into divine secrets!

Since we will be discussing the apocryphal Book of Enoch, we should address the reason that it was not included in the Bible. Most of us know that there were many books that were not included during the formation of the canonized Bible, either in the Hebrew or Christian scriptures. Some of the more interesting Christian scriptures are the Infancy Gospel of Thomas and the Protoevangelium of James, which talk about Jesus's life before he was twelve. Remember, the Bible has nothing to say about these "missing" or "hidden" years of Jesus, as they are sometimes called. Some of the most interesting and unusual stories of Jesus's childhood experiences come from the Infancy Gospel of Thomas, which is thought to have been written around the second or third century CE.

One story in this book tells how the child Jesus made some clay birds, and then brought them all to life. The book is filled with supernatural acts by the child Jesus—some are actually malevolent. For example, a boy takes some water from Jesus, which he had collected. Jesus is *not* happy about this, and curses the boy. Immediately the boy's body withers and dies. Another incident occurs when a boy bumps into Jesus by accident and again Jesus curses him and he also dies. These stories do not sound like something your minister or priest would recount during Sunday worship. You can see why this book, and others like it, did not make it into the biblical canon. They were obviously factious and had no historical or theological value.

One of the most bizarre stories about Jesus is found in the First Gospel of the Infancy of Jesus, also known as 1 Infancy. The entire story, about a man who was changed into a mule, is found in 1 Infancy 7:12–35. During one of their travels, Jesus and his mother were taken to a house to lodge for the night. When they arrived, they found several women weeping in the parlor. Before them stood a mule that these women were kissing and feeding. One of the ladies told Jesus and Mary that this mule was their brother, born of the same mother. After their father died, the sisters tried to find a suitable match for the brother. They said that

> a giddy and jealous woman bewitched him (using witchcraft) without our knowledge. And we, one night, a little before day, while the doors of the house were all fast shut, saw this our brother was changed to a mule, such as you now see him to be.[1]

They tell Jesus and Mary that they have consulted with wise men, magicians, and diviners but they have been of no service to them and could not restore him to his previous state. At this point Mary and Jesus took action and miraculously restored the man to his former state.

> Hereupon St. Mary was grieved at their case, and taking the Lord Jesus, put him upon the back of the mule. And said to her son, O Jesus Christ, restore (or heal) according to thy extraordinary power this mule, and grant him to have again the shape of a man and a rational creature, as he had formerly. This was scarce said by the Lady St. Mary, but the mule immediately passed into a human form, and became a young man without any deformity.[2]

One infancy story that is dear to my heart is sometimes referred to as "Joseph's bad carpentry." It seemed that if Joseph, in his woodworking, made something too short or too long, Jesus would either lengthen the wood or shorten it miraculously.

> And Joseph, wheresoever he went in the city, took the Lord Jesus with him, where he was sent for to work to make gates, or milk pails, or sieves, or boxes. And as often as Joseph had anything in his work, to make longer or shorter, or wider, or narrower, the Lord Jesus would stretch his hand towards it. And presently it became as Joseph would have it. So that he had no need to finish anything with his own hands, for he was not very skillful at his carpenter's trade.[3]
>
> 1 INFANCY 16:1–16

I wish I had Jesus with me during my shop classes in high school!

There are also other books that tell additional stories about Jesus after his death and resurrection—the Gospel of Nicodemus and the Gospel of Bartholomew, for example. They explain and give details of the death of Jesus not found in the Christian scriptures. The Gospel of Nicodemus, which is thought to have been written in the fourth century CE, is composed of the acts of Pilate and Christ's descent into hell. It gives a much more detailed account of Jesus's trial before Pilate and his crucifixion. It also mentions "limbo," an early and medieval Catholic teaching. (Limbo is the place that children go if they die before being baptized, because they are not thus freed from original sin. The church eventually rescinded this teaching.)

Enoch is also mentioned in the Gospel of Nicodemus. The idea that Enoch and Elijah will return to Earth at the end times comes from this gospel. The story is found in Nicodemus 20:1–4. The story continues from the previous chapter in which Jesus had descended into hell (remember the Apostle's Creed?)—he gathers together all his saints and Adam, and then ascends from hell with all of them.

> . . . and all the saints of God followed him. Then the Lord holding Adam by the hand, delivered him to Michael the archangel: and he

led them into paradise, filled with mercy and glory; And two very ancient men met them, and were asked by the saints, Who are ye, who have not yet been with us in hell, and have had your bodies placed in paradise? One of them answering, said, I am Enoch, who was translated by the word of God: and this man who is with me, is Elijah the Tishbite, who was translated in a fiery chariot. Here we have hitherto been, and have not tasted death, but are now about to return at the coming of Antichrist, being armed with divine signs and miracles, to engage with him in battle, and to be slain by him at Jerusalem, and to be taken up alive again into the clouds, after three days and a half.[4]

Thus this story states that Enoch and Elijah, the only two people translated to heaven, will return in the end times to battle the antichrist. There are also many other books that were not included in the current Bible—if you're interested in reading more about these, please see the bibliography. There were many criteria that the early church used to accept a book into the canon, and I believe that many of these other books should have been included, because they would have enriched the current Bible. Again, politics and personal bias played a major factor as to which books were included and which were not.

As mentioned in this long list of apocryphal Hebrew scriptures, we actually come to several books that are attributed to the patriarch Enoch. We will discuss these in detail in the next two chapters. The apocryphal Book of Enoch that we have been referring to is actually two separate books, called 1 Enoch and 2 Enoch. In addition to relaying the detailed story of the seventh patriarch who was taken up to heaven by the angels, they also tell us about spiritual realities not found anywhere else in biblical literature.

It turns out that when Enoch was taken up to heaven, he witnessed many different spiritual realms and was told to write about these experiences. That was his role or mission and, I believe, the reason he was taken up and not allowed to die. We do not know the original authors who wrote these books of Enoch, but scholars date their composition from about 300 BCE to the first century CE. Thus it is obvious that they were not written by the actual patriarch Enoch, who was the great-grandfather of Noah, but by a later writer who either made this information up or who had access to ancient legends and stories about Enoch that may have been passed down to him by an oral lineage.

We will discuss some of the details and what scholars know of these books, especially the second Book of Enoch, as that is the one most relevant to us. One very interesting story in these books is the fall of the "Watchers"—the angels that rebelled against God. These Watchers descended to Earth and married mortal women, and the children they produced were known as Nephilim, or giants. They are mentioned in the standard Bible in Genesis 6:1–4 (ESV) as the sons of God.

When man began to multiply on the face of the land and daughters were born to them, the sons of God saw that the daughters of man were attractive. And they took as their wives any they chose. Then the Lord said, "My Spirit shall not abide in man forever, for he is flesh: his days shall be 120 years." The Nephilim were on the earth in those days, and also afterward, when the sons of God came in to the daughters of man and they bore children to them. These were the mighty men who were of old, the men of renown.

In addition to mating with human females, they also taught humans forbidden knowledge:

Moreover Azazyel taught men to make swords, knives, shields, breastplates, the fabrication of mirrors, and the workmanship of bracelets and ornaments, the use of paint [i.e. makeup], the beautifying of the eyebrows, the use of stones of every valuable and select kind, and all sorts of dyes, so that the world became altered. Impiety increased; fornication multiplied; and they transgressed and corrupted all their ways. Amazarak taught all the sorcerers, and dividers of roots: Armers taught the solution of sorcery. . . .

1 ENOCH 8:1–4[5]

In addition to this fantastic tale of the Watchers, what is most interesting to me is that 2 Enoch, also known as the Book of the Secrets of Enoch, has a remarkable description of the seven heavens, which Enoch was allowed to travel through and visit. Enoch is taken up to each of these heavens, in order, from the first to the seventh, and he writes about what he sees. Each heaven has its unique description and its unique dwellers. For example, the second heaven is the abode of the fallen angels who rebelled against God. The seat of paradise is located in the third, and the throne of God in the seventh. (In chapter 3, we will go with Enoch through each of these seven heavens and read his descriptions of them.)

We have stated that these books of Enoch were not written by the prophet Enoch himself, but were created or composed by a different author generations later, who used the name of the prophet Enoch to give the book some prestige, a common practice at that time. But was the later composition based on some strands of true history that were passed down from one generation to another by oral tradition about something extraordinary that happened to the patriarch named Enoch? I believe that this may be the case. If indeed there *was* a real and original Book of Enoch, it has been lost to mankind. Perhaps a copy will be discovered one day, just as the Dead Sea Scrolls and other ancient books were hidden away and preserved in the desert sands and in caves, to be found later in history.

In the next two chapters, we will discuss what we know about the apocryphal books of Enoch and how they may be related to the Book of Enoch that Dr. Dee received from the angels in the sixteenth century.

2

THE APOCRYPHAL
BOOK OF ENOCH

Let's take a detailed look at the reference to Enoch in Genesis from the last chapter. The KJV version reads, in Genesis 5:24, "And Enoch walked with God, and he was not; for God took him." Most Christian Bible commentaries interpret these verses to mean that Enoch was translated or taken bodily to heaven, and thus did not experience physical death—yet this is not stated explicitly in these verses.

What does it really mean that God took him? Did he take him to heaven for good, or temporarily; in body or in spirit, or in both? Would he eventually return to Earth, and was this a real experience or a vision? There are many possibilities that would fit. So, why does almost everyone interpret this to mean that Enoch was translated (taken to heaven physically) for good?

There is another reference to Enoch in the Christian scriptures, in the Book of Hebrews, and the author explicitly states that Enoch was translated.

> By faith Enoch was *translated* that he should not see death; and was not found, because God had *translated* him: for before his translation he had this testimony, that he pleased God. (My italics.)
> HEBREWS 11:5 (KJV)

Since most Christians believe that the Bible is the word of God, and since the Book of Hebrews in the Christian scriptures states that Enoch was translated, most accept this as being what actually happened to him. But what if this was just the personal interpretation of the author of Hebrews, and not divine revelation? Either way, these verses in Genesis do not plainly say that this is what happened to Enoch, and it is still left open for interpretation. Remember, the author or authors of Genesis are different than the author or authors of Hebrews, and they both lived at different times.

We mentioned previously that besides Enoch, another person in the Bible was supposedly translated directly into heaven without dying—that person is the prophet Elijah.

> And it came to pass, as they still went on, and talked, that, behold, there appeared a chariot of fire, and horses of fire, and parted them both asunder; and Elijah went up by a whirlwind into heaven.
>
> 2 KINGS 2:11 (KJV)

In fact, some believe, as we have mentioned, that both Enoch and Elijah will return to Earth at the end times. Some creative writers have speculated that Elijah was taken up in a UFO (a chariot of fire).

Now, how much do we really know about the non-canonical or apocryphal Book of Enoch, which is sometimes referred to as a pseudepigrapha?* Let's take a minute to discuss some terminology. Apocrypha means hidden, esoteric, spurious, or of questionable authorship or authenticity. Such books are not considered sacred or inspired, and thus not part of the accepted canon of a religious denomination. From a Protestant's perspective, apocryphal books are the seven books that are included in the Catholic Bible but not included in the Protestant Bible.

---

*Pseudepigrapha are books falsely attributed to historical figures; examples beyond the Book of Enoch include the Second Epistle of Peter, which is falsely attributed to the historical Saint Peter. The biblical Pseudepigrapha were written from 200 BCE to 200 CE.

They are the books of Tobit, Judith, Wisdom, Ecclesiasticus, Baruch (1 and 2), and Maccabees, and also additions to the books of Esther and Daniel.

These seven books and additions are not considered apocryphal books to Catholics, but are part of their sacred and accepted canon of forty-six Hebrew scriptures, as opposed to the Protestants' thirty-nine. To Protestants, the pseudepigrapha are those additional books (not counting the seven Catholic books) that were also not included in their Bible. The canonical or accepted books are thus different for different Christian sects.

For example, even though the Book of Enoch is not included in the canon of most Christian Bibles, it *is* included in the canonical books of the Ethiopian Orthodox Church. Thus, whether a specific book is called canonical, apocryphal, or pseudepigraphical depends on the frame of reference of any given religion. Catholics call the Book of Enoch apocryphal, Protestants call it pseudepigraphical, and the Ethiopian Orthodox Church calls it canonical.

As we mentioned, the Book of Enoch is actually two separate books, 1 Enoch and 2 Enoch. (There is actually a third—3 Enoch—and it has a much later origin than 1 or 2 Enoch. It is believed to have been composed in either the fifth or sixth century, and its authorship is ascribed to Rabbi Ishmael ben Elisha, a high priest. This book is his account of his journey into the heavens. Since this is a book of much later and questionable origin, we will not focus on it.)

Authorship of 1 and 2 Enoch is ascribed to the prophet Enoch mentioned in the Bible, but, as we mentioned, this is unlikely. Enoch is only mentioned briefly in Genesis, in the letter of Jude, and in Hebrews. 1 Enoch was quoted occasionally by some of the early church fathers. Some looked favorably upon the book, as did Origen, Irenaeus, and Tertullian. Others were less favorable. During the fourth century, the church finally decided that it was not sacred or inspired, but actually heretical. After this time, it was lost for the next 1,500 years. Thus it never made it into modern Bibles. We now know about this book as several copies and fragments have surfaced in multiple languages over the last several hundred years, which we will discuss.

Complete manuscripts and fragments of 1 Enoch have been found in Ethiopic, Aramaic, Greek, and Latin, although there are very few Greek and Latin fragments. The only language in which a complete text has been found is Ethiopian. There is no consensus among scholars, but most believe that the original language of the composition of the book was probably Aramaic or Hebrew, or perhaps a combination of both languages.

Aramaic fragments have also been found in four different Dead Sea Scroll caves (caves one, two, four, and six). The fragments are small, and translation is difficult—but some of the more interesting fragments name the twenty chiefs of the fallen angels (4Q201), the miraculous birth of Moses (4Q204), and the giants mentioned in Genesis (4Q530).

1 Enoch is composed of five sections, and scholars believe the first section of the book (Book of the Watchers) is the oldest, and dates from about 300 BCE. The second part of the book (Book of Parables of Enoch) has the latest composition date at around the end of the first century BCE.

The five sections of 1 Enoch are titled:

1. Book of the Watchers
2. Book of Parables of Enoch
3. Astronomical Book
4. Book of Dream Visions
5. Epistle of Enoch

Scholars also believe that these five sections of 1 Enoch were originally independent works, each one having a different author and written at different times. They were each edited over a long period of time, and eventually some person or editor put them together into one book.

1 Enoch was rediscovered in the eighteenth century by the Scottish

traveler James Bruce. In 1773, he returned to his native Europe from his travels with three copies of this book, which he discovered in Ethiopia. All of the books were written in the Ethiopian language. Bruce kept one copy for himself, and the other copies were presented to the Royal Library of France and to the Bodleian Library at Oxford.

> Amongst the articles I consigned to the library at Paris, was a very beautiful and magnificent copy of the prophecies of Enoch, in large quarto; another is amongst the books of scripture which I brought home, standing immediately before the Book of Job, which is its proper place in the Abyssinian canon; and a third copy I have presented to the Bodleian Library at Oxford, copied by the hands of Dr. Douglas, the Bishop of Carlisle. The more ancient history of that book is well known. The church at first looked upon it as apocryphal; and as it was quoted in the Book of Jude, the same suspicion also fell upon that book. For this reason, the First Council of Nicea threw the Epistle of Jude out of the canon; but the Council of Trent, arguing better, replaced the apostle in the canon as before.[1]

It was not until 1821 that the first English translation was made and published by Richard Laurence, a professor of Hebrew at Oxford University. A revised edition was issued in 1883. (An interesting side note is that the famous theosophist H. P. Blavatsky, whose works have always been among my favorites, refers to the Laurence edition dozens of times in her book *The Secret Doctrine*. She must have found esoteric truths in it for her to quote it that much in one of her most important books. In fact, she explicitly states that the Book of Enoch is a kind of summary of the history of the third, fourth, and fifth root races of our Earth.

> The Book of Enoch, in short, is a *résumé*, a compound of the main features of the history of the third, fourth, and fifth races; a very few prophecies from the present age of the world; and a long retrospective, introspective, and prophetic summary of universal and

quite *historical* events—geological, ethnological, astronomical, and psychic—with a touch of theogony out of the antediluvian records. The book of this mysterious personage is referred to and quoted copiously in the *Pistis Sophia,* and also in the *Zohar* and its most ancient Midrashim (Rabbinical expositions on the holy books). Origen and Clement of Alexandria held it in the highest esteem. To say, therefore, that it is a post-Christian forgery is to utter an absurdity and to become guilty of an anachronism, since Origen, among others, lived in the second century of the Christian era, yet he mentions it as an ancient and venerable work. The secret and sacred name and its potency are well and clearly, though allegorically, described in the old volume. From the eighteenth to the fiftieth chapter, the visions of Enoch are all descriptive of the mysteries of initiation, one of which is the burning valley of the "fallen angels."[2]

In 1890, Robert Henry Charles published both a translation and commentary, which is even today considered to be one of the best (please find it listed in the bibliography). Aramaic fragments of the Book of Enoch were found among the Dead Sea Scrolls, and these were first published in the 1950s. The discovery of this book at Qumran was very significant, as it proved the antiquity of the Book of Enoch and also its popular use at Qumran.

2 Enoch, also called the Book of the Secrets of Enoch (a completely different book than 1 Enoch), was rediscovered at the end of the nineteenth century. Interestingly, it was discovered in the archives of the Belgrade public library by a Professor Sokolov. The book is in Slavonic, but most scholars believe that the original book was written in Greek, probably around the first century CE by an Alexandrian Jew, although some argue that it could have been written as late as the twelfth century CE. It has been debated whether the original author or authors were Jewish or Christian. Most of the extant texts that have been found are in Slavonic, and more than twenty manuscripts and fragments have been discovered of 2 Enoch, dating as early as the fourteenth century.

This book can be divided into four sections.

1. Enoch is taken by two angels and is transported to or passes through the seven heavens
2. Enoch enters the seventh heaven and comes face to face with the Lord
3. This section contains a list of instructions Enoch gives to his sons
4. This section outlines the priestly succession of Enoch

2 Enoch is of most interest to us since it describes Enoch's journey through the seven heavens—and maybe we can find some parallels that some, including myself, have experienced using Enochian Magic or meditations. In the next chapter we will go with Enoch as he travels through each of the seven heavens. But first I want to bring up an important question that you must be asking at this time.

Is there any relationship or dependence between the actual Book of Enoch that Dr. Dee received from the angels and the apocryphal Book of Enoch that we have just been discussing?

Let us list some specific points first.

1. We will assume that the book Dee received from the angels is the real Book of Enoch, the most holy book given to man by God and the angels. The angels stated this many times.
2. We will also assume that the real or historical prophet Enoch of the Bible also had the same or actual Book of Enoch, since the angels told Dee that this was the case. In fact, the angels considered Dee to be the second Enoch, as he would bring this information to the world again.

Let us ask this important question: What did the Enoch of the Bible have or experience that Dee did not? The answer is *the actual experience of the heavenly realms* as described in the apocryphal Book of

Enoch. Most, if not all, of the biblical commentators assume Enoch was physically taken up to heaven and never physically died because of his closeness to God (he walked with God), as we have mentioned above. It is possible that Enoch was temporarily, and not permanently, taken to the heavens to experience these revelations and to write about them for posterity—but he eventually returned to Earth in his physical body. It is known that some mystics may actually disappear physically when they travel to different realms. To a person seeing this, it would appear they were taken away, probably to heaven, and were not coming back. Here is another interesting thought: Did Enoch practice Enochian Magic, and was it so powerful that he disappeared during his trance?

If so, when he came back, he told others about this, and either he or they put these experiences in writing, or they were passed from one elder to another until strands of this story survived down through the ages, either in written or oral tradition. Eventually someone had the idea to put this story down in writing under the pseudonym of Enoch. They may have tried to piece together the entire story from these stands. How do we know that this writer or editor was not also inspired, and the angels helped him complete the story? Did he practice the magic also? Was this what came to us as the apocryphal Book of Enoch? Maybe the book isn't just a story made up around 200 BCE, but contains details of some of Enoch's actual experiences. Let's go a step further. Is it possible that this written book is an actual expression of the tables of Enoch that Dee received? Is there a link here that needs further exploration and research? I believe so.

Why did the apocryphal Book of Enoch last through the ages, and why was it preserved? Someone or some group felt it was important. Why did the Catholic Church incorporate its beliefs and theory of angels from this book? They must have felt it had divine inspiration, or at least did before the books of the canon were officially sanctioned.

Let us ask one more important question before we move on. Did Dr. Dee know about this apocryphal Book of Enoch and have access to a copy at that time? We do have copies of his list of the books that were in his library, and this book is not named—nothing at all in his catalog resembles the Book of Enoch. But in his diary, he makes some vague statements that he read about Enoch and his favor with God. Was he just referring to the description in Genesis, or did he have access to an extant copy of the apocryphal Book of Enoch? We can only guess.

So, let's now join Enoch in his travels through the heavens and determine what we may learn and experience from this.

3

ENOCH'S VISIONS
AND REVELATIONS

We know that there are two different apocryphal books of Enoch, 1 Enoch and 2 Enoch. 2 Enoch is also called the Book of the Secrets of Enoch. This book is the one of most interest to us, as it describes Enoch's travels and experiences through the seven heavens. The purpose of the Enochian meditation, which you will be taught later in the book, is to explore and (in a sense) travel through the thirty Aethyrs or heavens, so it would be appropriate and interesting to look at Enoch's experiences. I am asked many times if there is any relationship between the seven heavens of Enoch and the thirty Aethyrs of the Enochian system. I believe that this is possible, but I have no idea how I would divide up the thirty Aethyrs to correspond to the seven heavens. We must keep in mind that we really don't know if this apocryphal Book of Enoch has any historical shreds of truth regarding Enoch's actual travels. It may just be a completely facetious book created in the first century or later. Either way, it's still very interesting to learn what someone had to say about Enoch's travels through these heavens.

The book starts out by saying that Enoch the Just was chosen to be an eyewitness of the life above, or the experience of the heavens. I find an interesting parallel to the story of Dr. John Dee right at the beginning of the book. We have mentioned that Dee was a scholar and, in fact, one of the most—if not *the* most—intelligent and educated men alive at that time. Here, in the first sentence of 2 Enoch, Enoch is called Enoch the Just and, in addition to that, a wise man and a great man of letters. Thus, it seems that both were chosen to be messengers because of their advanced learning and knowledge. It is also interesting that another man of letters in the Christian scriptures, Paul, was taken up to the third heaven.

> I knew a man in Christ above fourteen years ago, (whether in the body, I cannot tell; or whether out of the body, I cannot tell: God knoweth;) such an one caught up to the third heaven.
>
> 2 Corinthians 12:2 (KJV)

Most scholars believe that Paul was actually writing this verse about himself. This verse may have referred to his vision on the road to Damascus that occurred earlier in his life, which is described in the book of Acts 9:1–9 and 22:6–11.

Getting back to the story of Enoch, it does state that Enoch was given this vision of the life above so that he could be a witness of these heavenly realms. The story begins when Enoch is 365 years old. He is alone in his house one night, sleeping in bed. Two men appear out of nowhere, and are shining like the sun. They call out his name. He awakes frightened (who wouldn't be), and they tell him not to be afraid, but that the Lord sent them to him to take him to heaven. They also tell him to tell his sons (Methuselah and Rigim) and others not to look for him until the Lord returns him to them.

The two men or angels take Enoch on their wings and carry him to the first heaven. He is brought in front of the elders, who are the masters of the stars. They explain to him the movements and the displacement of the stars. He is also told that these two hundred angels rule the stars and the constellations. The winged angels in this first heaven fly about. They also control the weather; Enoch says that they show him the treasuries of the snow and ice, and the storehouses of the clouds and the dew. The scene ends abruptly here, and Enoch is now brought by the two angels to the second heaven.

The second heaven seems to be concerned with the punishment of the apostate angels, who Enoch observes are under guard. They have been condemned and are weeping. Enoch asks who these weeping angels are, and is told that these are the apostate angels who did not obey the Lord's commands, but acted on their own will. Enoch feels very emotional about this and feels very sorry for them. The apostate angels then ask Enoch to pray to the Lord for them. Enoch is shocked that they would ask him, since he says, "Who am I, but a mortal man that he should pray for them?" (We will see that these fallen angels are referred to again in the fifth heaven.) In fact, Enoch says, "Who knows whither I go, or what will befall me? Or who will pray for me?" Now he is brought to the third heaven.

The third heaven is the location of paradise and hell, and contains the Tree of Life. He is first set down in paradise, and he says it is more beautiful than anything he could imagine. The trees are in full bloom, full of ripe fruit, and are beautiful. The place is permeated with a wonderful, fragrant breeze. The Tree of Life is located here, also, and its fragrance is indescribable. The entire place is so wonderful and blessed that it is beyond description. What I find interesting is that he says that the angels there continually sing to God with sweet voices. Most mystics throughout time talk about the music of the spheres or the planes where (as one advances on the higher planes of consciousness) they start to hear beautiful and indescribable music. The angels tell Enoch that this place is reserved for the righteous that endured hardships in life, who were just and who gave bread and clothing to the needy. They also lifted up those who had fallen, defended those who were wronged, and lived their life in the presence of the Lord and served him. This place was their eternal inheritance.

Next he is taken north of heaven, which he says is a very terrible and frightening place. There is every kind of torture and torment here, and dreaded darkness. No light shines here, but only a dark fire rising up, and cruel angels that have instruments of torture and torment and inflict torment without mercy. The angels tell him that this place is prepared for the impious and godless and those who work spells and incantations (i.e. black magic). These people steal the souls of men and grow rich from others through injustice and deceit. They do not help the starving and poor in need. It is interesting that the location of hell is in one of the heavens.

Enoch is then brought up to the fourth heaven by the two angels. This seems to be the realm of the sun, moon, and seasons. Enoch is shown the movements or displacements of the sun and the moon. I assume he is shown the secret of the astronomical laws of our solar system, on a more spiritual level. Unfortunately, he does not go into any more detail. He mentions that the sun's light is seven times greater than the moon's. Seven is a mystical number, so it may not be a quantitative relationship here, but an expression that represents something. He also sees four stars on the right and four on the left of the sun that move with it. Also, he sees angels flying before the sun with twelve wings each. These angels carry the heat and rays of the sun to the earth. He is also shown the movement of the moon. There is also a description of the cycle of the seasons. Now he is taken on to the fifth heaven.

In the fifth heaven, he observes another group of Watchers (different ones than the fallen Watchers in the second heaven). They are like men, but much bigger—in fact, they are bigger than giants. They are very sad and do not speak, but are silent. The angels explain to Enoch that these Watchers did not follow the other disobedient angels, who were their brothers that disobeyed the Lord and went down to Earth and defiled themselves with human women. This story is told in Genesis 6:1–6, as we have quoted before.

These Watchers are sad because their brothers (the fallen Watchers) were punished and are suffering in the second heaven. Remember, they were the ones that asked Enoch to pray to the Lord for them. Enoch tells these Watchers that he has seen their brothers who asked him to pray for them, and he has prayed to the Lord for them. Enoch tells the

Watchers not to brood but to resume serving the Lord, in case the Lord gets angry with them and condemns them also. The Watchers listen to Enoch's advice and they begin to serve the Lord, and go up into his presence. So, Enoch does a good deed by helping these angels.

In the sixth heaven, Enoch sees seven identical angels together that shine like the sun. They control and arrange the order of the celestial bodies (sun, moon, and stars), and bring order and harmony to all aspects of life in heaven. They also regulate and oversee all the angels who control the rivers, seas, seasons, time, vegetation, animals, and people of the earth. They are also the record keepers for the actions of all humans.

At this point, we come to the end of our journey and arrive in the seventh and last heaven. As you would expect, this place is filled with angels of all kinds and ranks, including archangels. It is so overwhelming to Enoch that he is afraid, and trembles. The Lord is here also, and is sitting on a throne and is worshipped by the heavenly hosts. The Cherubim surround the Lord's throne and sing in his presence. Enoch is so overwhelmed that he falls flat on his face. The Lord sends Gabriel to Enoch, who tells him not to be afraid, and to rise up and stand in the presence of the Lord.

Enoch comes into the Lord's presence and describes him as follows. The Lord's face was mighty and glorious, and Enoch does not go into any details, as he says, "Who am I to describe this?" The Lord then tells Enoch to stand in his presence forever (perhaps he is not going back to Earth?). The Lord tells the archangel Michael to take off Enoch's earthly clothes and dress him in glorious or heavenly garments, which he does. Enoch then looks at himself and realizes that he now looks no different than the glorious ones (the angels). Did the Lord turn Enoch into an angel? It appears so.

The Lord then summons one of his archangels (names differ in the different manuscripts), who is told to give Enoch a pen to write down all that happens in the heavens and on the earth. It takes the angel thirty days and nights to explain all these truths and mysteries to Enoch, and then another thirty days and nights for Enoch to write them all out (this recalls Enmeduranki, in the Sumerian Kings List, who was also initiated into the mysteries of heaven and earth). When Enoch is done, he has written 360 books. Could the legend of these books be related to the tables of Dr. John Dee? Now Enoch is allowed to go back to Earth for thirty days so that he can tell everyone in his family what happened to him. After that time, God will send for him and he will return to heaven for good.

The most important aspect of this story for me is the 360 books (some manuscripts have 366) that Enoch writes. Wondering if there were any relationship to Dee's Book of Enoch of forty-eight tables, I played around with these numbers, and other significant numbers related to Dee's tables, but could not come up with anything.

When Enoch is in the Lord's presence, he is told by the Lord that he has been given secrets that not even the angels have received. The Lord tells Enoch to take the books he has written and go back to his sons on the earth and tell them all that has been revealed to him. He is told by the Lord that his sons will pass the books that he has written to their children, and down from one generation to the other. These books will never be destroyed, even unto the end of time. The Lord will send two of his angels to Earth to guard and preserve these books so they will not be destroyed in the flood that is to come. He also tells Enoch that in the future these books will be revealed to the men of faith by the guardians of the earth. These books will be more highly valued and respected at that time than ever before.

Here we end our discussion of the apocryphal Book of Enoch and move on to the real Book of Enoch that Dee received from the angels.

4

DR. JOHN DEE
AND THE ANGELS

As mentioned before, it is important to realize that Dr. John Dee was probably one of the most intelligent and knowledgeable people alive in the world during his time. We have also mentioned that Dee was noted for his expertise in the fields of mathematics, cartography, navigation, cryptology, astronomy, and medicine, as well as many others. He is probably most famous for writing the preface to the first English edition of *Euclid's Elements of Geometry* (1570). He also gave many illuminating lectures on Euclid's geometry at universities all over Europe. Some attribute the revival of mathematics during the Renaissance to him. He also played a major role in the scientific revolution of that time, training many famous English explorers in navigation and cartography with his own state-of-the-art navigational equipment; many explorers came to him for lessons in its use. He also coined the term "British Empire," and advocated the expansion of the kingdom. For a more detailed biography, there are many good references listed in the bibliography.

After Dee turned fifty, he started to spend more time studying the occult and trying to contact angels. He believed that one couldn't find the answers to the highest mysteries through academic learning, but only by spiritual experience and contact with higher spiritual beings. The method he tried was called scrying; that is, looking into a crystal ball

Figure 4.1. Dr. John Dee

and seeing visions of other spiritual realms and angels. Unfortunately, he did not have the talent or ability to do this, but he met someone who did—Edward Kelley. Together, they succeeded in contacting angels in the 1580s, and Dee meticulously recorded all of this in his diary. Kelley definitely had the gift for scrying, and he and Dee soon became successful at invoking and communicating with the angels. Kelley's tool was a quartz crystal ball, and Kelley could both clairvoyantly see and hear the angels in the crystal.

The angels started out by giving Dee and Kelley instructions on building some ritual apparatus, like a table, ring, diagrams, symbols, and so on, for use in the communication process. After this (what I call communication apparatus) was completed, the angels were going to give them the Book of Enoch and something they named "Calls." The Calls were invocations that, if repeated, would act like keys to open up specific heavenly realms, which they called Aethyrs. Once an Aethyr was entered, its resident angel or governor could be contacted. Dee and Kelley were given the specific Calls for each of the Aethyrs and the names of the resident angels of each one. What's strange is that the angels explained very little in the way of details about the actual procedures for *using* the Calls. They only told Dee and Kelley that the Calls opened up the Aethyrs or heavens.

The angels told Dr. John Dee that the information they were conveying to him was the information or magical workings that God had previously given to the famous Enoch of the Bible. One can understand why Dee was so excited about receiving this information.

The story of Dr. John Dee and how he communicated with the angels is told in detail in my previous book, entitled *The Lost Art of Enochian Magic*. Once Dee established communications with the angels, they told him the story of the fallen angels and how they came to Earth and gave man black magic. The angels made it clear to Dee that this type of magic should never be used. They also told Dee that he would be the messenger of this lost knowledge of Enoch. He would be the second Enoch, and be given the original and now lost Book of Enoch.

Here is a part of that angelic communication to Dee regarding Enoch and Dee's role.

The Lord appeared unto Enoch, and was mercifull unto him, opened his eyes, that he might see and judge the earth, which was unknown unto his Parents, by reason of their fall: for the Lord said,

Let us shew unto Enoch, the use of the earth: And lo, Enoch was wise, and full of the spirit of wisdom. . . . And after 50 dayes Enoch had written: and this was the Title of his books, let those that fear God, and are worthy read. . . . Now hath it pleased God to deliver this Doctrine again out of darknesse: and to fulfill his promise with thee, for the books of Enoch: To whom he sayeth as he said unto Enoch. Let those that are worthy understand this, by thee, that it may be one witnesse of my promise toward thee. Come therefore, O thou Cloud, and wretched darkness, Come forth I say out of this Table: for the Lord again hath opened the earth: and she shall become known to the worthy.[1]

Dee would be the new Enoch and revealer of this wisdom to the world again. We can speculate as to why Dee was chosen to receive this information. He was the most knowledgeable person in England, and perhaps even the world, at that time. He was also an expert in cryptography, and this skill could help him interpret the angelic communications that were sometimes shrouded in mystery and codes. Dee also had a deep interest and passion for the occult, and would treasure and value such wisdom from the angels. He had the right attitude, as he did believe in the possibility of contacting angels and communicating with them. Thus, he had the perfect background, interests, and beliefs for this type of work. In addition, Dee had a love and passion for ancient manuscripts and rare books. Given that he had the largest private collection in all of Europe, he would treasure a sacred book like this.

In fact, one of Dee's ambitions was to create a state library of books and manuscripts in England. He presented a proposal to the Queen titled *A Supplication for the recovery and preservation of ancient writers and monuments.* Unfortunately, nothing came of Dee's proposal, so he decided to continue to collect and expand his *own* large library of books and manuscripts until it was one of the largest private libraries in Europe. It was estimated that Dee's library contained over four thousand volumes. I am sure that this was very important in his being chosen, since the angels wanted to make sure this information was preserved and passed down to future generations. Though we can only speculate why Dee was chosen, it seems that he was the perfect choice for the angels.

One last thing to consider is the following: Dee meticulously kept diaries, and it was important not only to preserve but to represent the exact transmissions of this information from the angels. They could count on Dee to be exact and accurate in his recording of this knowledge. Thanks to Dee and others who preserved this information throughout the centuries, it is still available to us today.

5

DR. DEE RECEIVES
THE BOOK OF ENOCH

What is the Book of Enoch that the angels gave or transmitted to Dr. Dee? It appears to be a set of about ninety-five large tables. Let us first look at what these tables are actually composed of, and how the transmission process took place.

Each table was composed of forty-nine rows and forty-nine columns. This would yield 2,401 empty squares or cells (49 × 49 = 2,401). Each of these cells was filled in with a letter or a number, or was left blank. The angels would have to communicate the exact letters for Kelley to place in each of these empty cells or squares. The final product was ninety-five tables, each containing 2,401 cells filled with letters or numbers. (Multiplying 95 by 2,401 gives 228,095 spaces.) Thus the angels had to specify over 200,000 letters or numbers to fill each of the empty cells. Actually it was less than that, since in some of the tables only every other cell was filled in—but, in general, we're talking about a large number of letters and numbers to be transmitted from the angelic world to our world. The other issue was that the angels told them that they had to complete these tables in forty days, and they actually did. The task commenced on March 29, 1583, and culminated on May 6, 1583, exactly thirty-nine days later.

So, how exactly were these tables transmitted to Dee? We know that Edward Kelley, Dee's scryer, could both see and hear the angels, most likely clairvoyantly. They could transmit information to him by sight, sound, or both. At first, it appears that an angel pointed to a letter on his set of tables with a rod, simultaneously pronouncing the letter. Kelley saw the letter and also heard the pronunciation clairvoyantly, and then wrote it down. Later, the angels, in order to speed up the process, did not pronounce the letters, but only pointed to them with the rod, and Kelley would say them out loud. It is interesting that Kelley could not read the letters until some supernatural fire or energy flashed into his head and he went into some kind of trance. This happened many times during the transmission of the tables. When the energy left his head, he came out of the trance and could no longer read or understand the letters. Here is the description, from Dee's diary, of what actually happened:

A voyce: Read.

EK: I cannot.

Dee: Then there flashed fire upon EK agayne.

A voyce: Say what thow thinkest.

EK: My hed is all on fire.

A voyce: What thow thinkest, euery word, that speak.

EK: I can read all, now, most perfectly.

Kelley goes on to read the letters that the angel points to. At the end of the session, it appears Kelley comes out of the trance as the fire from his head goes back to where it came from.

Dee: The fire cam from EK his eyes, and went into the stone againe. And then, he could not perceyve, or red one worde.[1]

Either Dee wrote the letters down on his sheet of paper as Kelley pronounced them or Kelley wrote them down himself. If Kelley wrote them down, then why would he repeat the letters out loud? Was it to verify to the angels that he had identified the correct letter without making any mistakes? The tables are in Kelley's handwriting, so either he wrote them down initially or, if Dee did, then Kelley eventually recopied them, and that is the version we have today. We will discuss this later, but for now, the important point is that the angels did communicate the information to complete the tables.

The angels also made another request of Dee and Kelley. They were instructed to eventually rewrite the tables, replacing the Latin letters with the Enochian equivalent of those letters (see the Enochian alphabet in figure 5.1). It appears that they never did this, or if they did, the location of these tables, if they exist, is not known.

According to the angels there are forty-nine tables, but only forty-eight were given to Dee and Kelley. The first table was never given, since the angels said that it was to be only of God, and too powerful and sublime for man to know or comprehend. The angel Nalvage explains why the first one was not given to them.

I finde the Soul of man hath no portion in this first Table. It is the Image of the son of God, in the bosom of his father, before all the worlds. It comprehends his incarnation, passion, and return to judgment: which he himself, in flesh, knoweth not; all the rest are of understanding.[2]

The angel Nalvage tells Dee about the importance of this information.

Unto this Doctrine belongeth the perfect knowledge and remembrance of the mysticall Creatures.[3]

The angels also made some strong statements regarding the forty-eight tables. They said it was the most important book ever given to man, and has been called the Book of the Speech of God. This book, they were told, will restore the knowledge that God originally had

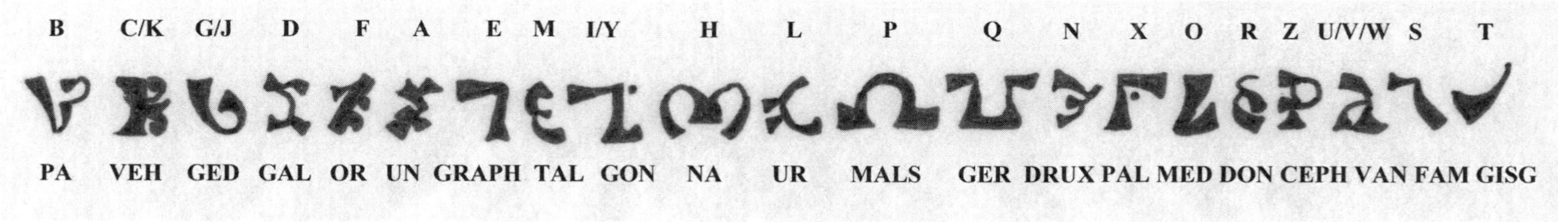

Figure 5.1. The twenty-one characters of the Enochian alphabet. This alphabet, which Kelley traced, appears on the last page of the Book of Enoch (i.e., the tables), as shown on page 216. I've redrawn these letters with our alphabet on top and the name of each letter underneath.

given to mankind, but was lost. The angels also imply that it may have something to do with the end times and be responsible for bringing in a new era or age to our planet. Here are some extracts of the angels' words regarding these tables, which I have modernized where appropriate:

> You have 49 Tables: In those Tables are contained the mystical and holy voices of the Angels: dignified: . . . which pierceth Heaven, and looketh into the Center of the Earth: the very language and speech of Children and Innocents, such as magnify the name of God, and are pure. . . . These Tables are to be written, not by man, but by the finger of her which is mother to Virtue. . . . These things and mysteries are your parts, and portions sealed, as well by your own knowledge, as the fruit of your Intercession.[4]

> Out of this, shall be restored the holy bokes, which have perished even from the beginning, and from the first that lived. And herein shall be deciphered perfect truths from imperfect falsehood, True religion from false and damnable errors . . . ; which we prepare to the use of man, the first and sanctified perfection: Which when it hath spread a While, THEN COMMETH THE ENDE.[5]

The following is the most important passage regarding the true purpose of the tables:

> I am therefore to instruct and inform you, according to your Doctrine delivered, which is contained in 49 Tables. In 49 voyces, or callings: which are the Natural Keyes, to open those, not 49, but 48 (for One is not to be opened) Gates of understanding, whereby you shall have knowledge to move every Gate, and to call out as many as you please, or shall be thought necessary, which can very well, righteously, and wisely, open unto you the secrets of their Cities, and *make you understand perfectly that contained in the Tables.* Through

which knowledge you shall easily be able to judge, not as the world doth, but perfectly of the world, and of all things contained within the Compass of Nature, and of all things which are subject to an end.[6] (My italics.)

Thus opening the gates (by using the Calls) and going into the cities (Aethrys) allows one to then unlock the forty-eight tables. (In chapter 9, I give these Calls and instructions on how to use them with the Book of Enoch.)

The forty-eight Calls allow us to enter the Aethyrs, and once inside we are taught the secrets and how to read the tables, as instructed by the angels.

As we have discussed previously, when Kelley was in a trance, he was able to understand the tables. When the trance ended, he had no idea of their meaning. So, maybe the trance is referring to an altered state of consciousness like that produced with God's meditation.

Here is an important statement by the angel Gabriel about the tables:

Thus hath God kept promise with you, and hath delivered you *the keys of his storehouses:* wherein you shall find (if you enter *wisely, humbly,* and *patiently*) Treasures more worth than the frames of the heavens. . . . Therefore, now examine your Books, Confer *one place with another, and learn* to be perfect for the practice and entrance. See that your garments be clean.[7]

These tables and Calls are worth more than the frames of the heavens. This should tell you how precious this information is. You must also be prepared spiritually, as the angel says: enter *wisely, humbly,* and *patiently.*

The angels also made these statements about the tables:

Wherein, they will open the mysteries of their creation, as far as shall be necessary: and give you understanding of many thousand secrets, wherein you are yet but children; for every Table hath his key: every key openeth his gate, and every gate being opened, giveth knowledge of himself of entrance, and of the mysteries of those things whereof he is an inclosure.[8]

One is one: neyther is, was or shalbe known: And yet there are just so many. These have so many names, of the so many Mysteries, that went before. . . . O what is man, that is worthy to know these Secrets?[9]

This boke, and holy key, which unlocketh the secrets of god his determination, as concerning the begynning, present being, and ende of this world, is so reverent and holy: that I wonder (I speak in your sense) whie it is delivered to those, that shall decay: So excellent and great are the Mysteries therein conteyned, above the capacitie of man. . . . One thing excepted: which is the use thereof. Unto the which the lord hath appointed a day.[10]

The angels told Dr. Dee not to read this book aloud or try to understand it until the appointed time.

God shall make clere when it pleaseth him: & open all the secrets of wisdome whan he unlocketh. Therfore Seke not to know the mysteries of this boke, tyll the very howre that he shall call thee.[11]

Before we end this chapter, let us address these tables. I have referred to them as ninety-five tables. As stated previously, these actual tables, which are in the handwriting of Kelley, are currently in the collection of the British Library. I have a complete printed set, and they are definitely composed of ninety-five tables, each with a forty-nine × forty-nine grid pattern. Here's what's confusing. The angels refer to these tables as the

set of "49 Tables" (notice I used a small t for tables when I was referring to one table, or page composed of one forty-nine × forty-nine grid
pattern but a large T for Tables when the angel referred to them as 49
Tables). But as I mentioned, there are actually ninety-five tables, or
ninety-five pages of tables, in the British Library collection. I believe
the answer lies in a statement made by an angel. The angel "Ile," who
later delivered the Calls to Kelley, said that:

Every Table containing one whole leaf. . . .[12]

Book collectors know that one leaf is composed of the front and
back. So, one leaf would contain two tables, one on the front side of
the paper and one on the back side, referred to as the verso. For simplic-
ity's sake, let us just assume that there were actually ninety-four tables
instead of ninety-five. (I explain on page 39 why this assumption is jus-
tified.) If we divide ninety-four by two, we get forty-seven.

The angels had also said that the first Call could not be given as
it is too heavenly or spiritual to be given to man. So, Dee and Kelley
were only given forty-eight and not forty-nine tables. But if we only
have forty-seven tables, we are still short one table.

To confirm that only forty-eight tables were transmitted to Kelley
and Dee, let us read the angels' own words, and the actual vision of the
book that Kelley observed on March 24, 1583. Notice that the angel
uses the word "leaves" and not pages, or two pages per leaf, and he also
makes it clear that there are forty-eight total leaves.

First, Kelley observes that the angel "Medicina Dei" is holding
a book, and says: "All the *leaves* are like gold and it seems that they
were written with blood, not dried. . . . There are forty-eight *leaves*."
(*Italics* are my emphasis, and I have modernized the English.) The angel
Medicina Dei then says:

One . . . shall not be known.[13]

The above definitely shows that the Book of Enoch, which the angel was holding, has forty-eight and *not* forty-nine leaves, and that they are leaves and not pages.

Let's look in detail at the complete Book of Enoch, which Dee called *The Liber Loagaeth* and which is kept in two collections known as Sloane 3188 and 3189 in the British Library. The entire book consists of:

- Twenty-eight pages of Enochian words, including a table of nine lines of forty-nine letters per line on the last page (see appendix B, illustrations 1–28 on pages 93–120)
- Ninety-five pages of individual tables (see appendix B, pages 122–215)
- One page with the twenty-one characters of the Enochian alphabet (see figure 5.1 on page 33 and appendix B on page 216)

The twenty-eight pages of Enochian words (from Sloane 3188) are in groups of (let us call them) paragraphs. Each paragraph is labeled with a number, and each paragraph is composed of forty-nine separate Enochian words. Each word is supposed to fit into one space of a forty-nine × forty-nine table (instead of one letter). Because Kelley and Dee could not fit these words into the allotted space, they wrote them out in sentence format. Thus the forty-nine words in paragraph one would fill in the forty-nine columns in row one. Paragraph 2 also has forty-nine Enochian words that fit into each column on row 2, and so on. So when we get done with the forty-nine paragraphs of forty-nine words each, we have completed filling in the forty-nine rows of a table. The first twenty of these twenty-eight pages of Enochian words make up the front side of the first leaf.

Pages twenty-one through twenty-eight make up the back side of the first leaf. The first paragraph on page 21 was incorrectly labeled 2 and is shown crossed out and correctly labeled 1 (see appendix B, page 113). Dee renumbered all the subsequent paragraphs on these pages, crossing out the numbers in the squares and writing the correct number to the left. The last numbered paragraph of forty-nine words is numbered 40 (remember the 41 in the square is crossed out). Thus we have forty of the forty-nine rows needed to complete the table on the back side of the first leaf.

Also on the twenty-eighth page is a table of nine rows by forty-nine columns, each of which is filled in with a letter (see appendix B, page 120)—a foreshadowing of the individual tables that make up the balance of the Book of Enoch. These additional nine rows complete the table of forty-nine rows and forty-nine columns on the back side of the first leaf.

So with these twenty-eight pages we now have two tables, one on the front side of the first leaf and the other on the back side of the first leaf—the first of the forty-eight leaves of tables that comprise the Book of Enoch. Following these twenty-eight pages are the ninety-five tables (Sloane 3189). For the moment let us assume there are ninety-four tables and not ninety-five. You will see why shortly.

The ninety-four tables, plus the two additional tables that are made up of the pages of Enochian words in each cell, equal ninety-six pages of tables. If we divide this by two, we get *forty-eight leaves*. This is consistent with the angel's statement that there are forty-eight tables or leaves. But there are actually ninety-five pages of tables in the British Library copy, and I assumed for our calculations that there were only ninety-four.

I went through the British Museum scans in detail and, lo and behold, I found a page that was reproduced twice. Whoever did these scans many years ago must have thought that the first scan of this page was too light, so they scanned it again but did not discard the extra scan. That is my opinion of what probably happened. So, if you eliminate the duplicate page, you now actually wind up with ninety-four tables! (If you want to verify this, the duplicate page is numbered eighteen on the manuscript in the British Library.)

6

THE DISCOVERY OF
THE HIDDEN
FORTY-NINTH TABLE OF
THE BOOK OF ENOCH

The angels are clear in explaining that in reality there are forty-nine tables, but that only forty-eight were given to Dee and Kelley. The first table was never given since the angels said that the soul of man has no portion in this table and that this table neither is, was, or shall be known. I believe that the angels changed their mind at a later date, and Dee was given the first table, and I believe that I may have discovered and deciphered it. I tried to reconstruct it according to the directions Dee was given by the angels, and I included this table in my previous book, *The Lost Art of Enochian Magic* (pages 165–66), because it is possible that someone else may discover its meaning or shed some light on it. I have a theory about why the angels initially told Dee and Kelley that they would not give them this table and apparently later changed their minds (see chapter 10). I also want to verify that I have correctly identified and interpreted this information. I will give all the details on this now.

It's very interesting that the best way to hide something is to put it right out in front of everyone. People always miss the obvious. I believe that this is the case with the first table. It's mentioned at the beginning of the Casaubon diaries.* I had missed it every time I read this section.

I looked at this section in the original Dee handwritten diaries, and in the margin, which was not reprinted by Casaubon, was the statement by Dee titled "The 49th Table." (Whether it is labeled number one or forty-nine is irrelevant, it is the missing table that was not originally given to Dee.) So Dee believed that what he was given in this section was the last or missing table. Below I have reproduced this section from the Casaubon reprint so we can discuss it. The description in the Casaubon reprint begins on page 19.

Gal [Galvah]: Touching the Book, it shall be called Logah: which in your Language signifieth Speech from GOD. Write after this sort LOAGAETH: it is to be sounded Logah.[1]

This is a very important sentence—it gives three main points about the book:

1. Gives the title of the book as "LOAGAETH"
2. Says it means "Speech from God"
3. States how it is to be pronounced: "Logah"

Also, in the margin of Dee's handwritten diary, but not in the Casaubon reprint, is the drawing that appears on page 42 (see figure 6.1).

This word is of great signification, I mean in respect of the profoundnesse thereof. The first leaf (as you call it) is the last of the Book. And as the first leaf is a hotchpot without order; So it signifieth a disorder of the World, and is the speech of that Disorder or

---

*Dee's diaries were first typeset and published by Meric Casaubon, D.D., in 1659, many years after Dee's death in 1609.

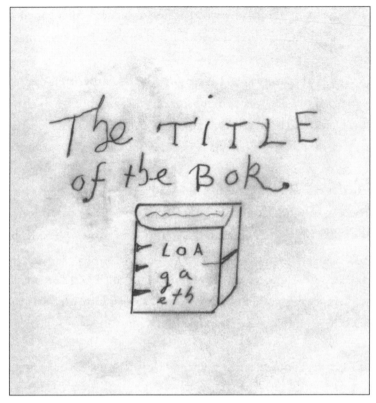

Figure 6.1. From Dee's diary, marginal drawing of the picture of
the book with its title (redrawn by John DeSalvo)

Prophesie. Write the Book (after your order) backward, but alter not
the form of letters, I speak in respect of the places.

E. K. Now a beame shooteth through him from the Stone and
so through his head and out of his mouth, his face being from E. K.
toward Δ*. . . . Write the forty-nine. You have but forty-eight already.
Write first in a paper apart.[2]

It is clear that this is the forty-ninth table. The angel Galvah says
to Dee that he already has the forty-eight, and this is the forty-ninth.

---

*Causabon used the triangle symbol to let us know when Dee was speaking instead of
writing out what Dee was saying.

He is also to write it and keep it separate from the forty-eight tables for some reason.

> E. K. Said that Galvah her head is so on bright fire, that it cannot be looked upon: The fire so sparkleth and glistreth as when an hot iron is smitten on an Anvil, & especially at the pronouncing of every word. It is to be noted also that upon the pronouncing of some words, the Beasts and all Creatures of the World every one shewed themselves in their kind and form: But notably all Serpents, Dragons, Toads, and all ugly and hideous shapes of beasts; which all made most ugly countenances, in a manner assaulting E. K. but contrariwise coming to, and fawning upon Galvah. It is to be noted also that by degrees came a second beame, and a third beame of light into Galvah from the Stone, and all the three together appeared: the third participating of the other two.

> The second beame came at the word Larb, pronounced; when also Frogs and Serpents appeared, &c. The third beame upon the word Exi pronounced. Note also, that the manner of the firy brightnesse was such, and the grisely countenances of the Monsters was so tedious and grievous and displeasant to E. K. that partly the very grief of his minde and body, and partly the suspecting the Creatures to be no good Creatures, neither such grievous sights necessary to be exhibited with the Mysteries delivering unto us, had in a manner forced him to leave off all: But I again with reasonable exhorting of him, and partly the providence and decree Divine, wrought some mitigating of his grief and disquieting.[3]

The words are so powerful that upon pronouncing them strange things happen, as indicated above. Again, in the margin of Dee's diary, and not in the Casaubon reprint, is a clear note indicating that this is the forty-ninth table (see figure 6.2 on page 44).

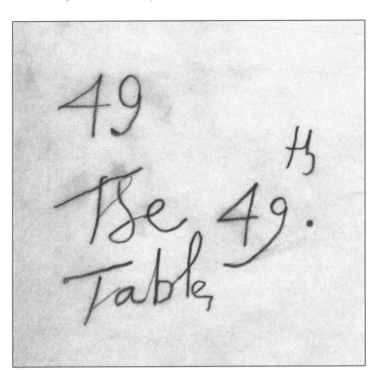

Figure 6.2. From Dee's diary, marginal notation of
the forty-ninth table (redrawn by John DeSalvo)

Also, in both the Casaubon book and the Dee diaries, of course, are
the actual letters of the table (figure 6.3 below).

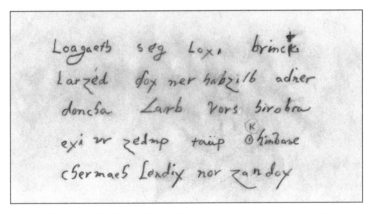

Figure 6.3. From Dee's diary, handwritten letters of
the forty-ninth table (redrawn by John DeSalvo)

Gal . . . [Galvah] These are these seven.

Dee: Blessed and praised for ever be He who is one and three: and whom mighty ministers or governours do incessantly glorifie.[4]

Dee: What shall I do with these twenty-one words now received;

Gal: . . . There are onely the words of the first leaf.

Dee: I pray, how shall I bestow them, or place them.

Gal: . . . In them is the Divinity of the Trinity.

The Mysterie of our Creation.

The age of many years.

And the conclusion of the World.

Of me they are honoured, but of me, not to be uttered: Neither did I disclose them my self: For, they are the beams of my understanding, and the Fountain from whence I water.

Dee: I beseech you, how shall I write these names in the first leafe.

Gal: . . . They are to be written in five Tables, in every Table twenty-one Letters.[5]

Here is the key. There are five tables of twenty-one letters each, which would total one hundred and five letters. If you go back to figure 6.3 and count the letters, you come up with the following number of letters in each line shown below. You have to make sure you don't miss the "I"s, which are almost hidden. This is what I initially got of the total of the letters in each of the five lines.

20–21 (I'm not sure if the last letter should be
    there or is crossed out.)

24

21

24

23

Totals 112 or 113

This is seven or eight more letters than it is supposed to be.

Now I tried to study the first line in detail and decided that the last letter should be there, and is not crossed off. If that is the case, we now have 113 letters. That is eight more than we should have. Then it dawned on me: The first word is not part of the table. It is the *title* of the table, *Loagaeth,* which is eight letters long. So if we subtract that, we wind up with exactly 105 letters and twenty-one words.

Dee: How shall I place the five tables upon two sides: three in the first, and two in the second, or one in the first, and four in the second, or how else?

Gal: . . . As thou seest cause.

Dee: Shall I write them in Letters of Gold?

Gal: . . . The writing hath been referred to thy discretion with collours, and such things as appertain to the writing thereof. Upon the first side write three Tables, and on the second two.

Dee: How, thus?[6]

Here, Casaubon has a blurred series of dots and lines that you cannot make out. But if you go to the Dee diaries, you see what is shown in figure 6.4. Thus, there are seven columns of the three letters in each row. This is how I originally set up the tables. I made three tables on the front of the paper and two on the back or verso as the angel indicated.

Gal: . . . Set them down, I will direct thy judgement.

Dee: When, now?

Gal: . . . Not now.

E K: She is gone.[7]

All of the above is happening on Tuesday, June 18, 1583. The next day, Wednesday, June 19, 1583, the angels imply a different setup. It appears Dee received some information about this that was not recorded. He sets the tables up in triangles, and not three × seven rectangles.

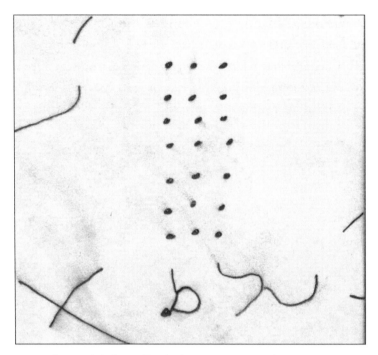

Figure 6.4. From Dee's diary, the setup of the letters
(redrawn by John DeSalvo)

Dee: I have assayed divers wayes to place the five Tables, on the two
sides on this first leaf; Is it to your likeing as I have done it, in the
five little Triangles?[8]

So before this communication, Dee tried other ways of organizing
the words, and decided the triangle setup was the best. We do not know
why he settled for this, but the angel said it was sufficient. Does that
mean that it was OK, but not the best way?

Gal: . . . As concerning the setting down of the five Tables. It is sufficient as it is done.[9]

So, if you look at the figures on pages 48 and 49, you can see the setup of the 105 words: twenty-one words in each triangle, three triangles in the front and two on the back or verso.

Thus, I believe that what I have constructed from the Dee diaries is the missing table of the Book of Enoch, and that we now have the complete *Book of 49 Tables.*

Figure 6.5. Reconstruction of the front side of the forty-ninth table

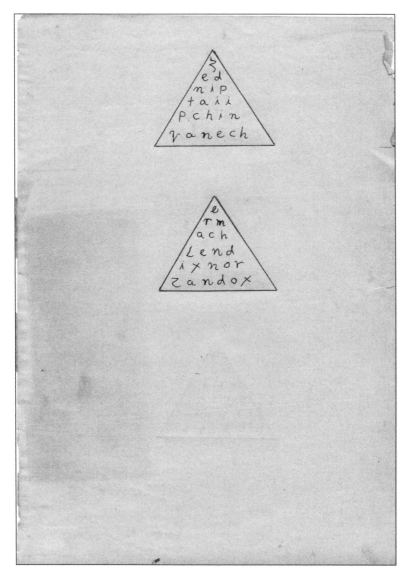

Figure 6.6. Reconstruction of the back side of the forty-ninth table

1

THE MISSING SET OF TABLES IN DEE'S HANDWRITING

As we have discussed, the tables of the Book of Enoch that are in the British Library, and which we have reproduced in appendix B, are in the handwriting of Edward Kelley. I propose that there may be a missing set of original tables in Dee's handwriting. As we have previously discussed, the tables were transmitted to Dee and Kelley in the following way. The angel pointed to a letter on his table or globe (at first the angel also repeated it out loud or clairvoyantly to Kelley, but later abandoned this way and only pointed to it). Kelley would see what it was and then repeat it out loud. Now we don't know if Kelley wrote the letters down on his set of tables as he saw them, or Dee wrote them down on his set after Kelley repeated them out loud. I personally believe that Dee wrote it down—what reason would Kelley have to repeat them unless someone was listening to copy them? That would have been Dee. A different reason why Kelley repeated the letters out loud was to verify to the angels that he saw the letters correctly. I favor the first reason.

What evidence do we have for this? We do know that MS 3189 (i.e. the ninety-four tables with the several pages of Enochian words at the beginning) are all in Kelley's handwriting. So if Dee initially wrote them down, Kelley must have made a later copy from Dee's original.

We know that the first page of the first leaf of the tables is not in MS 3189, but in MS 3188, which is in Dee's handwriting. We also have the back page of this leaf, also in MS 3188, and it's also in Dee's handwriting. The first side of the first page was not transferred to MS 3189, i.e. Kelley did not copy this page, but only the back side of this first leaf, which is in MS 3189 in Kelley's handwriting. Thus we have a duplicate copy of the back page of the first leaf, one in Dee's handwriting in MS 3188 and one in Kelley's handwriting in MS 3189.

I have studied Dee and Kelley's handwriting, and I believe that I can distinguish each fairly easily. There are certain characteristic letters that I use to identify each one, especially the "E"s (see figure 7.1). We have to ask if there are additional tables in Dee's handwriting. The answer is yes. In the preface of Meric Casaubon's *A True and Faithful Relation,*

Figure 7.1. The top script is from MS 3189 in Kelley's handwriting.
The bottom script is a representation of Dee's handwriting
(redrawn by the author) from the sample table in Casaubon's book.

Casaubon states that there are many tables at the back of these diaries, and that he will only reproduce one of them for this book, as it would cost too much to reproduce all of them; he also didn't think that they were significant.

The one that is in the 1659 book can be compared with the identical one in MS 3189, which is in Kelley's handwriting. Guess what? The one in Casaubon's book is in Dee's handwriting, not Kelley's. I realize that this was redrawn by the engraver of the plate, but he must have traced or followed Dee's characteristic handwriting and the way he formed letters. He must have used Dee's original drawing of this table. So, I believe that the tables in the back of Dee's spiritual diaries that Casaubon was referring to were the *original* ones drawn by Dee, all in Dee's handwriting. Besides a copy of this one table, the rest are all missing or destroyed. We only have the one that Casaubon decided to reprint.

There is also a discrepancy between the table in the Casaubon book with the same table in MS 3189. There appears to be more information on the Dee table. The title of the table is longer, with additional Enochian words. Did Kelley abbreviate and leave things out as he copied Dee's original tables? Is the MS 3189 Kelley copy that we currently have in the British Library not a true and complete copy? Is there anything missing that would change the supernatural effects of these tables? We won't know unless we eventually recover the missing Dee tables.

Let us try to follow the provenance of these tables. Fifty-four years after Dee died, some manuscripts of his were discovered—in a most interesting way. After his death, the furniture from his home at Mortlake was sold. Over the years, the items made their rounds from one owner to another. (I doubt the owners knew that it was the furniture of Dr. Dee.) A particularly interesting piece, a wood chest measuring about four and a half feet long, had several different owners, until something extraordinary was discovered about it by Robert and Susannah Jones. They bought the chest in approximately 1643, and it remained with them for the next twenty years. In about 1662, they decided to move the chest to a new place in their home, and during the process of moving it heard something rattle inside.

Robert Jones explored the bottom of the chest with a piece of iron, and found a crevice that opened up to a secret compartment. Inside this secret drawer were five unknown manuscripts by Dr. Dee, and a rosary chaplet made of olive wood. Unfortunately, the Joneses didn't realize the significance of what they had found, and the maid used some of the manuscript to wrap pies in and light fires. (I shudder to think how many manuscripts were destroyed by the Joneses' maid. Some have estimated that a half dozen manuscript books of Dee's were lost to the world forever.) Robert and Susannah eventually realized that the remaining manuscripts in their possession might be valuable, and removed them to a place of safekeeping.

Several years later, Robert died and Susannah remarried a Thomas Wale, who was a good friend of the well-known antiquarian scholar and book collector Elias Ashmole. (Ashmole was also a Freemason and very interested in the occult and metaphysics.) Robert decided to show Ashmole the papers. Ashmole realized their importance at once and obtained them from Robert, eventually passing them on to the British Library. (Ashmole's antiquarian collection, in fact, now makes up a significant part of the British Library.) Due to Ashmole's insight and generosity, we are now privy to these previously unknown manuscripts of Dr. John Dee, which are highly significant to the world of magic and may otherwise have been lost to the world.

We know that the original Dee tables were not in the secret compartment of his chest, since the chest did not come to light until after Casaubon published his book in 1659. The secret compartment with the manuscripts of Dee was not discovered until 1662, three years after Casaubon published his book. So, if Casaubon claims there are tables in the back of his book, they were never in the chest. In fact, the catalog of the chest does not include any description of these tables.

We really do not know the provenance of MS 3189, except that there is a note that says that this was the original manuscript in Edward

Kelley's handwriting. It belonged to the Cotton Collection, as stated in a note by Elias Ashmole.

Here is the most likely provenance. It appears that some of Dee's manuscripts were purchased by Sir Robert Cotton some time before his death in 1631. His son, Thomas Cotton, inherited these manuscripts. One set of manuscripts that we know of for sure was the diary that Casaubon published entitled *A True and Faithful Relation*. Cotton gave Casaubon access to the diary to transcribe and publish. I also believe that MS 3189 and the original Dee tables were part of this manuscript collection owned by Cotton. Elias Ashmole, eleven years (1670) after Casaubon published his book (1659), borrowed some of these manuscripts from Cotton. Thus they eventually ended up in the Ashmole collection and were eventually donated to the British Museum some time in the eighteenth century.

Since I believe both sets were together, it is possible that the Dee set has been lost or is labeled incorrectly somewhere in the British Library. There is another set, Sloane 2599, which is in Elias Ashmole's handwriting. Thus, he copied one of the sets of tables.

I therefore believe that there is a missing set of tables in Dee's handwriting which were the original or first ones drawn. Maybe this set will come to light some day.

8

SUBJECTIVE
EXPERIENCES
OF THE
BOOK OF ENOCH

How do you write a chapter about something that no one can clearly understand? The angels never explained the use or application of these tables of Enoch that were transmitted to Dee and Kelley. Dee never recorded anything in his diary regarding these tables that could give us any insight into how to use them. All we have are some cryptic statements from the angels about how important they are, and that this is the most important book given to man by God.

There are several possibilities:

1. The angels did give Dee instructions and detailed information about them, and this information has been lost. It is possible that some of the diary pages that were hidden in the chest and burned by the maid may have contained some information about this. It is also possible they are still hidden in some unknown place, perhaps in some other furniture of Dee's, some private collection, or in the British Library itself.

2. The angels were going to give Dee more information on their

use, but Dee and Kelley broke off the communications before the angels could give them this new knowledge.

3. Maybe the use of these tables was not given *at that time* for a reason.

I favor the third hypothesis for the following reason. It appears that the angels told Dee not to use this information unless they gave him the go ahead. There is no indication in any of his diary notes that he had the go ahead. I believe that the details on how to use the tables of Enoch were withheld from Dee and would be revealed at a future time. What that time is, no one knows. Maybe the time is now, and someone will solve this mystery, because the tables are now being reprinted for the first time and made accessible to the world. Your guess is as good as mine.

All we can do in this chapter is to look at what we have and make some observations. Maybe the key to all of this is in the tables themselves, and if we are creative and observant, we can find it and unlock their treasures.

I would like to share one of my experiences meditating with the Book of Enoch.

I experienced this when I was exploring the Twenty-second Aethyr during one of my Enochian meditations. As I was meditating, I entered a very deep state and I strongly felt the presence of God and the holiness of this Aethyr and his angels.

I saw all of the forty-nine tables (not just the forty-eight) floating in space, and it appeared that each leaf was separated from the next one by about an inch. Then the hand of God appeared, and his finger brushed or touched the first leaf, and it moved toward the second, and the second brushed the third, and so on and so forth. This was similar to dominos falling in slow motion. As each leaf hit the next one, something like letters or possibly notes came out from the leaves. They were numerous, and floated majestically in the air.

A good way to visualize this is by considering forty-nine very dusty pages of a book. If you fan the book, dust flies into the air. In this case it wasn't dust that came out, but letters. They moved and floated in a beautiful harmony, almost like a symphony. I knew this symbolized the creation of the universe by God. His finger brushing the first leaf was like the OM point or the Big Bang, which began everything. His finger was the Word of God (John 1:1). God only touched the first leaf and as his hand moved or fanned over the rest of the leaves, the wind that he produced from the hand motion moved the rest of them in a domino effect. This wind represents the "wind of God" mentioned in Genesis 1. The wind was hovering over the deep before creation began. Some people translate the Hebrew word for wind as Holy Spirit. So if this wind was the Holy Spirit of God, it was now taking over to finish the process of creating the universe. In my vision, all three persons of the Godhead were present: the Father, the Son, and the Holy Spirit. Notice that God only touched the first leaf, and no others. This is why the first leaf was so holy. This vision is consistent not only with Christianity in that the three aspects of God were present in the creation, but also Egyptian mythology. The Egyptian god Thoth was considered the tongue of god, in which the will of god was translated into speech. He has also been compared to the Logos or the Mind of God. In addition, he was the Egyptian god of magic and writing. He was considered to be the scribe of the gods and was credited with inventing the alphabet.

The letters coming out of the pages would be consistent with a cosmology where Thoth ruled as a god. He was the god who originated all things; the Egyptians believed that he was responsible for making all of the calculations for the establishment of the universe, including the stars, the planets, the earth, and everything they contained. It's very interesting that his female counterpart Ma'at controlled the movement of all things in the universe, and was the force that maintained creation—in other words, the wind.

In Crowley's vision of the Twenty-second Aethyr, an angel plays a pipe and, according to him, the music is wonderful. The angel stops playing and moves his fingers in the air, which leaves a trail of fire of many colors. There is some similarity between this and my vision of God moving his finger in the air and fanning the forty-nine tables. Crowley also seemed to see visions of the creation and dissolution of the universe. In my vision, I only beheld the creation. (Keep in mind I didn't read Crowley's description before I explored the Twenty-second Aethyr.) I was very grateful to the angels for revealing the vision of the Twenty-second Aethyr to me. It was one of the most sublime revelations I have ever received in my exploration of the Aethyrs.

In addition, I was told by the angel of that Aethyr that the key to the tables is in the first leaf—the one composed of paragraphs of Enochian words that were supposed to fit into the forty-nine × forty-nine grid patterns.

If you recall, an entire Enochian word would be placed in the cell in the first two tables instead of a single letter, so Kelley had to write out the words in a long string (they would not fit into the small cell area). The angel told me that the ninety-four tables should also be read as a string of Enochian words. That is, start with row one, column one, and list all the letters together until the end of that row, and at that point there should be forty-nine letters. Continue with the next row, until all the 2,401 letters are written out, one after another. I was told to do this for each table.

I said, "How will I know how to separate the words, since it would be just a string of letters?" He said, "When you look at the tables it will be apparent." I had no idea what he meant. So I started looking at a scan of the tables on my computer and enlarged them so I could read each letter, which was not easy, as the tables are very messy and the handwriting difficult to discern. As I was attempting to write down each letter in each cell, I noticed small commas and sometimes periods between groups of letters. I assume that's what the angel was referring to when he said, "It will be apparent."

I was totally surprised, because I'd studied these tables numerous times and never noticed the very small commas or periods. After I wrote out a few lines and separated the letters using commas to create words,

I tried to read them. It's interesting that the words *did* sound like the Enochian language. Unfortunately, not all the tables have these commas and periods, so there may be other clues regarding how to separate the characters into words. I'm in the process of investigating this further.

If you will recall, another hint I received was that at the top of each table is a title in the Enochian language, which, of course, no one has been able to interpret. I had been told that these were an important key in that they were *not* used in producing the Calls. Maybe they tie in somehow with the string of letters forming the words. I continue to research this, as well.

9

INSTRUCTIONS FOR MEDITATING USING THE BOOK OF ENOCH

Unfortunately, the angels never gave Dee or Kelley any instructions for using the Book of Enoch in any ritual or practical matter. In fact, they did not want Dee to use it until they gave the go ahead, and we don't know if they ever did. So, all we are left with is the book without any instructions for its use or for deciphering its mysteries. I believe one practical way to use it is with the Enochian meditation that I have taught in my previous book, *The Lost Art of Enochian Magic*. It seems that the angels said that once one enters the Aethyrs, they will help instruct you and open the keys to understanding the Book of Enoch.

The following is the most important message regarding the true purpose of the tables. On pages 76–77 of the Casaubon 1659 edition, we have the following communications between the angel Nalvage, Dee, and Kelley, which took place on Thursday, April 12, 1584, while they were in Poland.

I'm therefore to instruct and inform you, according to your Doctrine delivered, which is contained in 49 Tables. In 49 voyces, or callings: which are the Natural Keyes, to open those, not 49, but 48 (for One isn't to be opened) Gates of understanding, whereby you shall have knowledge to move every Gate, and to call out as many as you please, or shall be thought necessary, which can very well, righteously, and wisely, open unto you the secrets of their Cities, and make you understand perfectly that contained in the Tables. Through which knowledge you shall easily be able to judge, not as the world doth, but perfectly of the world, and of all things contained within the Compasse of Nature, and of all things which are subject to an end.[1]

Thus opening the gates (by using the Calls) and going into the cities (Aethrys) allows one to then unlock the forty-eight tables.

The forty-eight Calls allow us to enter the Aethyrs, and once inside we're taught the secrets of how to read the tables as instructed by the angels. The angels had emphasized that the role of the tables is central, but this had passed by me. I had been focusing on the Calls exclusively, because the tables didn't seem to serve any additional purpose that I could figure out. But apparently the entire purpose of entering the Aethyrs (which the Calls allow us to do) is to unlock our understanding of the tables.

So, one of my approaches is to do the Enochian meditation with the Book of Enoch on my lap, and once I enter an Aethyr and contact the governors or angels there, to ask them for understanding and wisdom regarding the book. I have decided to give the Enochian meditation instructions in this chapter, but recommend you obtain my other book, *The Lost Art of Enochian Magic,* which has more details and a CD of the pronunciations.

Specifics on the Enochian Meditation

The Enochian meditation technique uses no ritual equipment or props, except this book and a candle (which is optional). You should be able to accomplish the process in about thirty to forty minutes and, hopefully, get results the first time you do it. I had results my first time and continue to get results almost every time I do the technique.

Anyone with psychological problems, however, should not attempt to perform magic or this meditation. Too many people have gotten into trouble this way. They should first resolve their issues with the help of a licensed psychologist or psychiatrist. You must have a stable mind and, in a sense, a normal psyche to do magic. In fact, Israel Regardie, one of the most famous of the Golden Dawn magicians, felt that someone should undergo a long period of counseling before they even begin the practice of magic.

In the Enochian meditation, there are thirty Aethyrs we can explore, one by one, by conducting separate sessions for each. The usual procedure is to start at the Thirtieth Aethyr (the lowest or closest to the earth and farthest from God) and work your way up to the first (the highest one spiritually or the one that's closest to God). We may not be able to enter all of them, and how far we get may depend on our level of spiritual development and awareness, which is as it should be.

Even though I believe the following meditation is safe and helpful, I want to state that the author and the publishers of this book are not responsible for the effects or results of this technique. I suggest that you be sure to follow the correct procedures. Also, please know that this meditation isn't necessarily for everyone; you have to decide whether or not it's right for you. The minimum criteria for performing the Enochian meditation are that:

- You don't have any physical or mental problems that could inter-fere or cause any problems for you.
- Your purpose in doing this is to become closer to God and to experience his peace, knowledge, and wisdom—and not for any selfish, material reason.
- You follow the specifics of the procedure and learn them well before you attempt to modify the meditation to your own indi-vidual needs.

The entire meditation should take thirty to forty minutes if it's not rushed. It should be done with devotion and love. I like to think that I'm "on holy ground" when I do it.

The Lesser Banishing Ritual of the Pentagram

You will perform the Lesser Banishing Ritual of the Pentagram (LBRP) both before and after the Enochian meditation. Employing the LBRP is a way to purify your environment and protect yourself from any negative energies or entities.

The LBRP only takes a few minutes to do. It's extremely important that, as with any magical procedure, you treat the LBRP with respect and reverence. You're dealing with forces that we know little about. Just because your motives may be pure doesn't necessarily mean you will be protected from the consequences of using it. The LBRP is so ancient that no one really knows where it originated; it has lasted through eons of time because it's so effective. Almost every time I do the LBRP, I feel extreme peace and quiet, and the atmosphere around me seems pure.

The Enochian Meditation—Step by Step

The meditation is divided into three parts as follows.

Part One—Preparation and Preliminaries
This consists of the initial setup of the area you will be meditating in, the conducting of the preliminary visualizations and prayers, and an enactment of the Lesser Banishing Ritual of the Pentagram, which is comprised of the Kabbalistic Cross and the Pentagram of White Light. This normally takes five to ten minutes.

Part Two—The Enochian Meditation Itself
This consists of reading aloud the entire Enochian Call and meditating on the governors' names (the angels in charge of the Aethyr you're trying to enter, experience, and explore). (See also appendix A.) Reading

the Enochian Call out loud is the main thrust of this meditation. (I suggest you don't meditate longer than fifteen minutes at first. You can increase the time after you feel comfortable with the procedure.)

Part Three—Ending the Meditation

This consists of thanking the governors or angels, reading the license to depart and the final prayer, and performing the Lesser Banishing Ritual of the Pentagram. This usually takes about ten minutes.

THE ENOCHIAN MEDITATION

Part One—Preparation and Preliminaries

Seat yourself comfortably in a chair near a lighted candle.

Find a quiet place where you will not be disturbed by anyone or by any phone calls. Sit comfortably in a chair and place a lighted candle near you. (Make sure the candle is in a stable position where you can see the flame clearly at all times and where it will not fall or cause anything near it to catch on fire. Never leave a candle unattended.) The candle helps you visualize the Light of God and connects you to that light.

Take a few minutes to relax and pray.

Look at the candle. Think of God and his presence within you. The light from the candle symbolizes the Light of God and connects you to him. Be natural, and approach this effortlessly. Don't force any thoughts or feelings. This is a time to take a few minutes to settle down and realize that you're doing this meditation to be present with God and the angels and to experience higher spiritual realms. Recite a favorite psalm or prayers to put you in a devotional mood.

Perform the White Light Visualization.

Say the following to yourself while visualizing the light. (Close your eyes to help yourself visualize better.)

May the white light surround me.

May the white light elevate me and put me in touch with my spiritual guides.

May the white light connect me with the Divine Light, the Light of God.

Do the Lesser Banishing Ritual of the Pentagram.
(Do this standing, and read the words out loud.)

First you will first do the Kabbalistic Cross, and then you will construct the Pentagram of White Light. (The Kabbalistic Cross is similar to the sign of the cross, but the words and directions are different.)

The Kabbalistic Cross

- Stand facing east.
- Visualize the Light of God coming to you and hovering over your head in a dazzling, radiant ball of light.
- Reach up with your right index finger and, touching this ball of light, bring it to your forehead and touch your forehead.
- Say or chant: AH-TEH (Unto Thee . . .).
- Move straight down and touch your chest or stomach and say or chant: MAL-KUTH (. . . the Kingdom . . .).
- As you move your finger to each part of your body, visualize the white Light of God moving with you—at the end, you will have a large cross over your body from the white light.
- Touch your right shoulder and say or chant: VEE-GE-BUR-AH (. . . and the Power . . .).
- Touch your left shoulder and say or chant: VEE-GE-DU-LAH (. . . and the Glory . . .).
- Finally, bring your hands together in front of you like in prayer and say or chant: LE-OL-LAM (. . . Forever . . .) AH-MEN.

I would suggest chanting, as it gives this ritual more life and energy. Also, do not repeat the English translations of the words given above in parentheses. They are just for your information.

The Pentagram of White Light

- Facing east, trace a pentagram in the air. The size doesn't matter, but I usually make it on the large side. I visualize it as a white, vibrant, dazzling light, or as a blue flame—use whichever you can visualize most easily. As illustrated in figure 9.1, start at the lower left side of the pentagram and move in the direction indicated.

Figure 9.1. Start at the lower left corner and trace the pentagram in the direction indicated until you come back to the starting point.

- When the pentagram is complete, thrust your right index finger (which you're using as your magic wand) in the center of the pentagram and say or chant: YOD-A-HAY, VAV-A-HAY.
- Turn and face south.
- Make the same pentagram again in the air (starting at the lower left side) and, when completed, thrust your right index finger in the center and say or chant: AH-DO-NAI.
- Turn to the west (notice you're going around a circle in a clockwise direction), trace the pentagram, and when completed, thrust your right index finger in the center and say or chant: E-HI-YAY.
- Turn to the north, trace the pentagram, and when completed, thrust your right index finger in the center and say: AH-GA-LA.
- Turn to the east. Don't trace a pentagram; just thrust your finger into the center of the pentagram you traced initially, thus completing a closed circle of four pentagrams, each one facing a cardinal

direction (east, south, west, and north). Visualize this circle and the pentagrams as a vibrant light surrounding and protecting you. These four incantations are names of God.

- Still facing east, stretch out your arms in the form of a cross, and chant the following:

Before me: RA-FAY-EL.

Behind me: GA-BRE-EL.

On my right: ME-CHI-ALE.

On my left: UR-REE-ALE.

   (You're summoning the four archangels of God—Raphael, Gabriel, Michael, and Uriel—for protection.)

- Keep your arms outstretched and continue by saying:

Before me flames the pentagram.

Behind me shines the six-rayed star.

- Repeat the Kabbalistic Cross once more. You're now done with the LBRP.

After you have completed the LBRP, remain standing and pause for a few minutes. Just soak in the peace and calmness, and then sit down. ⋅

Part Two—The Enochian Meditation Itself

Read the entire Enochian Call (below) out loud.

If this is the first time you're doing this meditation, and you want to begin in the Thirtieth Aethyr (which I strongly recommend), you will be saying the name of the Thirtieth Aethyr (TEX) after you say "Mā -drî -iax Ds praf" (as I've indicated below). You will then continue reciting the entire rest of the Call out loud (because it acts like a mantra, it is most effective if it's recited out loud by you). You can chant it if that makes you feel more in tune with it. The words are broken into syllables, and pronunciation marks are added to indicate long and short vowels. (Note: The straight line above the vowel indicates a long vowel: ā ē ī ō ū; the caret symbol above the vowel indicates a short vowel: â ê î ô û.)

The Enochian Call (The Call of the Thirty Aethyrs)

Mā-drî-iax Ds praf (Name of Aethyr, i.e. TEX) ch(k)īs Mi-cā-olz Sa-ā-nir Ca-ōs-go, od fī-sis Bal-zi-zras Ia(ya)-ī-da, Non-ca(sa) Go-hū-lim, Mic(Mīk)-ma A-do-ī-an Mad, I-ā-od Bli-ōrb, Sâ-ba-o-o-ā-ô-na ch(k)īs Lu-cīf-ti-as pe-rīp-sol, ds Ab-ra-ās-sa Non-cf(sf) Ne-tā-â-ib Ca-os-gi od Ti-lb Ad-phaht Dām-ploz, To-ō-at Non-cf(sf) Gmi-cāl-zô-ma L-rāsd Tōf-glo Marb yār-ry I-doi-go od Tor-zulp ia(ya)-ō-daf Go-hōl, Ca-ōs-ga Ta-ba-ord Sa-ā-nir od Chris-tê-os Yr-pō-il Ti-ō-bl, Bus-dir ti-lb No-aln pa-id ors-ba od Dod-rm(rum)-ni Zyl-na. El-zāp-tilb Parm-gi pe-rīp-sax, od ta Q(K)urlst Bo-o-a-pi-S. Lnib(Lmb)-m o-v-cho Symp, od Chris-tê-os Ag-tol-torn Mirc Q Ti-ōb-l Lel. Ton pa-ombd Dil-zmo As-pī-an, od Chris-tê-os Ag L tōr-torn pa-rāch A-symp, Cord-ziz Dod-pal od Fi-falz Ls-mnad, od Farg-t Bams O-ma-ō-as. Co-nīs-bra od A-uâ-vox To-nug, Ors-cāt-bl No-âs-mi Tab-gēs Levith-mong, un-chi(ki) Omp-tilb Ors. Bagel. Mo-ō-ô-ah ol cōrd-ziz. L ca-pī-mâ-o Ix-o-māx-ip od ca-cō-casb Go-sâ-a. Ba-glen pi-i Ti-ān-ta A-bā-bâ-lond, od fa-ōrgt Te-lōc-vo-vim. Mā-drî-iax Tor-zu O-ād-riax Or-ō-cha(ka) A-bō-â-pri. Ta-bā-ôr-i pri-āx ar-ta-bas. A-dr(dir)-pan Cor-sta Do-bix. Yol-cam pri-ā-zi Ar-co-a-zior. Od quasb Q-ting. Ri-pīr pa-a-oxt Sa-gā-cor(kor). vm-L od prd(pur)-zar ca-crg(cōrg) Aoi-vē-â-e cor-mpt. Tor-Zu, Za-Car, od Zam-Ran aspt Sib-si But-mô-na ds Sur-zas Tia Bal-tan. Odo Cicle Q-ā-a, od oz-az-ma pla-pli Iad-nâ-mad.

Meditating with the Governors' Names

When you have finished reading the Enochian Call, repeat the names of the governors of the Aethyr you're working in out loud, or silently (which I prefer). Start with the higher numbers first. Thus, if you're opening the Thirtieth Aethyr, you will pronounce the names of each of the four governors, beginning with the ninety-first governor (Dozinal), then the ninetieth (Advorpt), then the eighty-ninth (Gemnimb), and then the eighty-eighth (Taoagla)—all four of whom belong to this Thirtieth Aethyr (all of the other Aethyrs have three governors). Close your eyes and use whatever method you feel most comfortable with. You can move from one angel to the next when you feel moved to do so. I usually dwell on the name of one governor for a few minutes or longer, and then go to the next one for a few minutes—and so on and so forth. Again, I prefer to do all of this silently. If you need to open your eyes to read the names of the governors listed in appendix A, that's fine. Eventually, you will know them by heart, and not have to refer to the book.

Stay with one Aethyr for each session. For example, don't mix the governors of the Thirtieth Aethyr (Tex) with those of the Twenty-ninth (Rii), listed below. Also, you don't have to use the governors' names as a continuous mantra. I like the example of going into a room and calling out the name of a friend. You keep calling him until he comes to you, and then you don't need to call his name anymore. When I feel the presence of a governor, I usually stop repeating his name. However, if you want to keep repeating them, that's fine, too. I've done it that way and it's very effective. This is your personal meditation, and you need to experiment to see what's right for you.

30. TEX
91. Do-zī-nal

90. Ad-vorpt

89. Gem-nimb (mmb)

88. Ta-ō-â-gla

29. RII
87. Gom-zī-am

86. O-drâx-ti

85. Vas-trim

See appendix A (pages 79–81) for a complete listing of the thirty Aethyrs and their corresponding governors.

🌿 Part Three—Ending the Meditation

When you're done repeating the names of the governors, take a few minutes to relax and come out of your deep rest.

This is important, since your body has been in a deep trance state for fifteen to twenty minutes, and you need at least two or three minutes to readjust. Just stop thinking of the governors' names, and you will gradually come back to your normal state. You can also thank the spirits mentally for their help.

Thank the Spirits (using your own words).
Thank the governors for appearing to you, spending time with you, and guiding you through their domain or Aethyr. You would do this for any friends who showed you around their town after a visit. I usually do this silently, but you can do it out loud if you prefer. Use your own words of thanks—whatever feels right to you.

License to Depart (Optional. Use if you feel the need
for this—read it silently or out loud.)
O spirits (name the governors here—for instance, Dozinal, Advorpt, Gemnimb, Taoagla), because you have been very ready and willing to come at my call, I hereby license you to depart to your proper place. Go now in peace and be ready to come at my call when requested. May the peace of God be ever continued between you and me.

Final Prayer (Optional.)
You can make up your own prayer, thanking God or saying whatever you feel moved to say.

Do the Closing Lesser Banishing Ritual of the Pentagram.
(Stand up and say it out loud.)
Sit down and rest for a few minutes before you get up and resume your activities.

Recommendations for the Enochian Meditation

Go slowly and enjoy the meditations. Don't try to analyze them while you're meditating. Just experience them—you can analyze them later on. It may take time to experience the Aethyrs in their fullest sense, but this is only logical. If you're exploring a new area or region, you're not going to see everything that there is to see the very first time. You also need to adjust to the new environment, and begin to use your new senses. Some people don't experience visual phenomena, but may feel the presence of *something*. You may have different experiences in the same Aethyr at different times. Again, everyone is unique—enjoy this new adventure.

I would suggest that you stick with the procedure I've outlined above for the first couple of weeks or longer. You can then modify it to suit your personal needs if you wish. Remember, magic is a science and an *art*. You're the artist, so tailor your meditation to suit your own personality.

10

REFLECTIONS AND
FINAL THOUGHTS

After studying, meditating, and researching these tables of Enoch for years, what conclusions can I draw? Let's list what we actually know about these tables at this point.

1. The angels never explained the meaning, use, or interpretation of these tables to Dee, or to Kelley in the conscious state. As we discussed, Kelley was at times illuminated with a beam of light, and this supernatural light allowed him to understand the meaning of the tables. Unfortunately, as far as we know, this information was never written down by Kelley, and when he came out of his trance, he did not remember any of it. It also seems that Dee did not write down anything that Kelley may have said while Kelley was in a trance.

2. Since the seventeenth century, as far as I am aware, no one has deciphered the meaning of any of these tables, not even the most famous Enochian magicians of all time, including Aleister Crowley and Israel Regardie. If you go through *The Complete Golden Dawn System of Magic* by Regardie, which is considered to be the bible of the Golden Dawn, you don't find anything about the tables other than a brief mention, which

is primarily concerned with the Enochian Calls and other aspects of Enochian Magic. Regardie had no idea how to interpret these strange tables. Aleister Crowley may have had a few insights during his period of exploring Enochian Magic and the Aethyrs, but he did not write down anything specific about them. So we cannot rely on these magicians—or any modern ones, as far as I know—to shed any more light on the meaning of the tables. Maybe there's someone out there who has deciphered them, and this information will eventually come to light.

3. In my Enochian meditations, I have been given some slight insight, and I have described these insights previously: the vision of the tables creating the universe and the angels giving me some idea how to use the tables by making Enochian words from the individual letters. This is interesting, but doesn't really give us more understanding of their use and meaning.

Based on these points above, I can come to only one conclusion. The angels want to keep the understanding and use of these tables secret until an appointed time. We know that the angels never gave Dee permission to carry out the Enochian Magic. He was supposed to wait until they gave him the go ahead, and as far as we know, this was never given. It's still debated whether the angels eventually gave him permission—but if so, Dee either never wrote this down in his diary, or the pages were lost.

I believe that the circumstances in which this information is now being made available to the public (i.e., the first time the tables in appendix B have ever been reprinted in a book) and the limited understanding that I have been given indicates that the time is near for the revelations of these tables to be made clear. There are currently so many books, movies, and articles about 2012 being the end date of the Mayan calendar. Yet I believe that this is not an end date, but the beginning of a new era—and maybe the tables play a role in this new beginning or era. This is just my speculation, but there are hints of this throughout the Dee diaries.

Some statements here and there about the antichrist, end times, and second coming of Christ seem to have little, if any significance. One that does, however, is a cryptic comment by the angel Gabriel about the second coming of Christ that I have found in Dee's diaries. These few sentences may give us some insight into the importance of the Book of Enoch and the Enochian Calls in the end times:

> Gabriel: So likewise, the Scriptures speak of the coming of Christ, but the day and hour, the Son of man knoweth not. But because in time to come, and for this *action* (the message of the highest), And assured, and infallible Doctrine (in respect that God appointed you no certain time), is necessary. For, for this cause you waver my brethren: and may lose the benefit of God his favour, and mercies. O weaklings examine the Prophets, look into the doing of the Apostles. There alwayes went a promise before the end: But the end was the benefit and fruit of the promise. Some alleadge Paul, some Peter, some Daniel: But in this case shall you alleadge the sayings of God, spoken in the spirit of truth by me Gabriel, the servant of the highest.[1]

What is so interesting is the placement of this statement in the diaries. It is just before the angel Nalvage gives Dee and Kelley the Thirty Calls of the Aethyrs, the most important information that the angels transmitted to Dee, in my opinion. This implies to me that the Calls and the tables may play an important role in the battle against the antichrist in the end times. In the statement above by Gabriel, the term *"action,"* which I have italicized, means all of the information the angels gave Dee in their communications. He is saying that this information that Dee has been given by the most high through the angels is infallible, and the exact date or time that all these things will happen will not be given to them. But he does say, "But because in time to come," implying that this information will be important for the future. Maybe I am reading too much into this, but I would conclude that the angel Gabriel is telling Dee the following points:

1. This Enochian Magic is infallible and from God.
2. Its use will be important in the end times.
3. No one will know when that date will be, not even Jesus.
4. Dee must not waver in his role as being the bearer of this information, just like the Prophets and the Apostles.
5. He must faithfully record this information of God, spoken to him through the angel Gabriel.

What an important calling from God. You can see why Dee was overwhelmed with all of this, and questioned his ability and wisdom to be the bearer of this knowledge to the world. This information has been stored in the British Library for hundreds of years, and only recently have reprints of the Dee diaries been published for the public eye. These tables in appendix B are the last of the Dee diaries to be reprinted—maybe this is an important event in the progression toward the end times.

It is interesting, and yet confusing, that angels would make a statement and then later either retract the statement or say something contradictory to it. For example, they first seem to imply to Dee that they would not give him the forty-ninth table and Call, since it was too holy for man to have. They then later transmitted the forty-ninth table, but not the Call. Maybe we need to read carefully to see what the angels really did say. Was there a contradiction or just a misunderstanding on our part? In this case, what I have discovered is that the angels say they will not give Dee the Forty-ninth Call, but do not say they will *not* give him the forty-ninth table. So, when I discovered the forty-ninth table in his diary and reconstructed it, it was not contradictory to anything that the angels had said.

This occurs elsewhere. One of the more important statements where there seems to be a contradiction is regarding the end times. The angels made it clear several times that no one knows the date of the end times, even Jesus Christ (see above). Then, it appears that a specific date is given in another section of the diaries that the angels had transmitted to him. Let's see what the angels had specifically stated about the end times.

In the Dee diaries that Casaubon reprinted, and the ones we are most concerned with here, in which there are more than eight hundred handwritten pages, we find only a few important references to the end times and the antichrist. I believe the angels wanted much of this information hidden until the appropriate time, so this may be why the information was presented in a cryptic manner. Let's look at a very interesting message of the end times delivered by Gabriel to Dee on June 2, 1584.

> Gabriel: But in you two is *figured* the time to come: For many shall cleave unto the Lord, *even at* the first call: And many shall doubt of the Lord, and not believe him for a season. But as you two shall dwell in one Center (if you [yet] do look forward, and step right), *So shall the face of the whole earth be, for 800. one hundred and fifty years.* (For, *the fruit of* Paradise *shall appear,* that nothing may be on earth without comfort. For, lo, the first shall be last,) and it shall be a Kingdom without corruption. . . . For, his Kingdom shall have an end with misery. And these are the latter dayes. And this is the *last Prophesie of the World.*
>
> I have *chosen* you, to enter into *my barns:* And have commanded you to open the Corn, that the scattered may appear, and that which remaineth in the sheaf may stand. And have entered into the first, and so into the seventh. And have delivered unto you *the Testimony of my spirit to come.*[2]

In the margin of Dee's diary, he has 950 years, thus the "800. one hundred and fifty years" should be added together to equal this number. It says, "A figure of the time to come. 950. Years." Thus, if we add

950 years to the year in which this information was transmitted to Dee, which was 1584, we get the year 2534. According to the angel Gabriel, the fruit of paradise will appear in this year. So is this the date of the end of the world according to Gabriel? Will paradise be ushered in for all in 2534? No one is supposed to know the date of the end times, but we are given this calculation to arrive at that time. All I can do is present the information as I find it in the Dee diaries, give my simple interpretation, and leave it for others to verify or refute it. It is there for all to see.

I can't resist telling you about something interesting I found out about this number. I always like playing with numbers, even though it may not really mean anything. I was wondering if this number, 2,534, had any relationship to our DNA—since if the world ends, the human race ends. It turns out that *Homo sapiens'* 2,534 gene is the primary factor in the control of all cell growth. Without cell growth, cells die, and therefore the body dies.

I wonder if our demise will be the mutation of a life-supporting gene, and if all life will just die. That would be a different scenario for the end times than floods, earthquakes, meteors hitting the earth, and pole shifts, for instance.

One last thing I would like to bring up that has bothered me about the angels is something I have experienced several times. Let's say I'm working on a project and I need specific spiritual help or information at a certain time. I don't always receive it. Then, when the deadline for the project almost arrives, the angels give me the information I need. In fact, it is usually much more information than I expected. I was a little perturbed about this, and was asking them, in my meditation practice, why this happens.

They told me that people don't realize that angels have rules, guidelines, and limitations from God. They are not given unlimited time to carry out their responsibilities of transmitting information to a specific person. In fact, God gives them a specific window or time interval to carry out their mission. They must act within this time, not before and not after. The recipient also has to play his part and must, by free will, be ready and receptive to receive the message during this specific time interval. Thus, a message could be missed and never delivered because the person chose not to receive it, or was not receptive at that time. Once the interval of time passes, the message is lost, and there is not a second attempt to deliver it. So, even though I or someone else may think the time is right to receive the information we need, the time for the window to open has not yet arrived. I thought that this was a reasonable explanation, and am satisfied with it.

One of the main purposes of this book is to get this information to the public, and hopefully others may discover something important that will add to our understanding of these mysteries. If you would like to share any insights or discoveries with myself or others, I've set up a website at MyAngelMagic.com to post your comments and additional information. You can also e-mail me at drjohn@gizapyramid.com.

I conclude this book with the statement that I make in so many of my discussions, interviews, and talks about this subject as to when these mysteries may be revealed:

"Maybe the time is now!"

THE NAMES OF THE NINETY-ONE GOVERNORS OF THE THIRTY AETHYRS

In the Enochian meditation, there are thirty Aethyrs we can explore, one by one, by conducting separate sessions for each. The usual procedure is to start at the Thirtieth Aethyr (the lowest or closest to the earth and farthest from God) and work your way up to the first (the highest one spiritually or the one that's closest to God). We may not be able to enter all of them, and how far we get may depend on our level of spiritual development and awareness, which is as it should be.

The governors are the angels in charge of the Aethyr you're trying to enter, experience, and explore. You can move from one angel to the next when you feel moved to do so. I usually dwell on the name of one governor for a few minutes or longer, and then go to the next one for a few minutes—and so on and so forth. I prefer to do all of this silently. If you need to open your eyes to read the names of the governors in the book, that's fine. Eventually, you will know them by heart, and not have to refer to the book.

Note: The straight line above the vowel is a long vowel: ā ē ī ō ū; the caret symbol above the vowel is a short vowel: â ê î ô û.

30. TEX

91. Do-zī-nal

90. Ad-vorpt

89. Gem-nimb (mmb)

88. Ta-ō-â-gla

29. RII

87. Gom-zī-am

86. O-drâx-ti

85. Vas-trim

28. BAG

84. Ox-lô-par

83. Fo-cīs-ni

82. Lab-nix-p

27. ZAA

81. Or-pâ-nib

80. Ma-thu-la

79. Sa-zī-â-mi

26. DES

78. Baz-chim (kim)

77. Ni-Grā-na

76. Po Phand

25. UTI

75. Ran-glam

74. Ob-uâ-ors

73. Mir-zind

24. NIA

72. So-ā-gê-el

71. Chi (Ki)-alps

70. Or-câ-mir

23. TOR

69. Zax-â-nin

68. O-ni-zīmp

67. Ro-nô-amb

22. LIN

66. Cal-zirg

65. Pa-rā-ô-an

64. O-zi-daī-a

21. ASP

63. Vix-palg

62. To-ān-tom

61. Chris-pa

20. CHR (KAR)

60. To-tô-can

59. Par-zî-ba

58. Zi-L-dron

19. POP

57. O-mâ-grap

56. Aba-ī-ond

55. Tor-zōx-i

18. ZEN

54. Yal-pa-MB

53. Za-fâ-sai

52. Na-ba-ô-mi

17. TAN

51. To-câr-zi

50. Ay-dropt

49. Sig-morf

16. LEA

48. So-chī (ki)-al

47. La-vâ-con

46. Cu-carpt

15. OXO

45. Tas-toxo

44. No-ci-â-bi

43. Ta-hân-do

14. UTA

42. O-ō-â-namb

41. Vi-uî-pos

40. Te-dô-and (Tedoond)

13. ZIM

39. Do-cê-pax

38. La-pâ-rin

37. Ge-cā-ond

12. LOE

36. Am-briol

35. Ge-dô-ons

34. Ta-pâ-mal

11. ICH (ik)

33. Po-nô-dol

32. Us-nār-da

31. Mol-pand

10. ZAX

30. Ta-bī-tom

29. Co-mâ-nan

28. Lex-ārph

9. ZIP

27. Do-ān-zin

26. Cral-pir

25. Od-dī-org

8. ZID

24. Pris-tac

23. Tod-na-on

22. Zām-fres

7. DEO

21. As-pī-â-on

20. Ge-nâ-dol

19. Ob-mâ-cas

6. MAZ

18. Zir-zird

17. Vā-vâ-amp

16. Sax-tomp

5. LIT

15. Ti-ār-pax

14. No-cā-mal

13. Laz-dix-i

4. PAZ

12. Poth-nir

11. Ax-zī-arg

10. Tho-tanf

3. ZOM

9. An-dīs-pi

8. Vi-rō-chi (ki)

7. Sa-mâ-pha

2. ARN

6. Di-a-lī-û-a

5. Pa-cās-na

4. Do-âg-nis

1. LIL

3. Val-gars

2. Pas-comb

1. Oc-cô-don

THE COMPLETE BOOK OF ENOCH

(As Given to Dr. Dee by the Angels)

The complete Book of Enoch, which Dee called *The Liber Loagaeth,* is kept in two collections known as Sloane 3188 and 3189 in the British Library. We assume that the book Dr. John Dee received from the angels is the real Book of Enoch, the most holy book given to man by God and the angels. The angels told Dee that the information they were conveying to him was the information or magical workings that God had previously given to the famous Enoch of the Bible. Dee and Kelley were given the specific Calls for the Aethyrs and the names of the resident angels of each one. What's strange is that the angels explained very little in the way of detail about the actual procedures for using the Calls. They only told Dee and Kelley that the Calls opened up the Aethyrs or heavens.

The tables that follow (which were the basis for only part of one of the Calls) were transmitted character by character to Dr. John Dee and Edward Kelley by the angels. The sections of the complete Book of Enoch you will be seeing include:

- The front side of the first leaf—derived from twenty pages of forty-nine Enochian word paragraphs from the diaries of Dr. John Dee, written in his own hand
- The back side of the first leaf—made up of eight pages of forty-nine Enochian word paragraphs and one small table of nine lines of forty-nine letters per line, also in Dr. Dee's own hand
- Forty-seven tables—made up of ninety-four pages of individual tables representing the front and back sides of leaf 2 (Table 2), through leaf 48 (Table 48), transcribed by Edward Kelley

Each table is composed of a grid of forty-nine rows by forty-nine columns, which produces 2,401 small squares. Each of these small squares is filled in with either a letter, a number, or it is left blank (see figure A.1). The exception to this rule occurs on the front and back sides of the first leaf, where instead of each empty square being filled in with a letter, number, or left blank, it is to be filled in with an entire Enochian word. Over each table is a title in the Enochian language, which no one has yet been able to translate.

When you look at tables 2 through 48 on pages 122–215, you can see that each square is too small to fit an entire word (examples of length of some Enochian words are "daph, adaph, omixdar, and tardemah"). Because the words are too long to fit into the very small squares, the entries for the front and back of the first leaf table were written out into paragraphs, with forty-nine words in each paragraph (see figures A.2 and A.3 on pages 87 and 88).

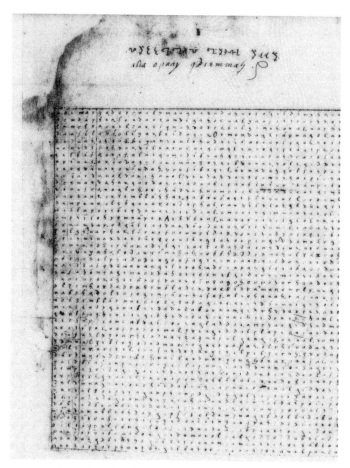

Figure A.I. The 49 x 49 grid produces 2,401 small squares.

The paragraph labeled 1 in figure A.2 contains the forty-nine words that would fill in the first row of forty-nine squares. Paragraph 2 contains forty-nine words that fit into each column on row 2. This pattern continues for all forty-nine paragraphs, each one containing forty-nine words, until the entire table of forty-nine rows would be filled in with all these words. As a result, one would end up with a grid of forty-nine × forty-nine, making up 2,401 squares, each filled in with a word. This table was never constructed because they could not fit the words into the small squares, but this is how it would have been.

Figure A.2 shows the paragraphs in the context of Dee's diary where the forty-nine Enochian words are surrounded by additional notations (see pages 92–120 for the full-size diary pages that comprise the front side of the first leaf). Figure A.3 shows a sample of the paragraphs that comprise the back side of the first leaf, which contain only the forty-nine-word passages without any additional diary notes. (See pages 121–28 for the complete set of paragraphs on the back side of the first leaf.)

There are twenty pages of forty-nine-word paragraph groupings from Dr. Dee's diary that make up the front side of the first leaf. On the back side of the first leaf we have another eight pages of forty paragraphs of forty-nine words. The first paragraph on page 21 (see fig. A.3 and also page 113) was incorrectly labeled 2 and is shown crossed out and correctly labeled 1. Dee renumbered all the subsequent paragraphs on these eight pages to correctly identify the passages on the back side. So when we review the numbered paragraphs, we must not reference the numbers crossed out in the squares but the corrected numbers that appear to their left. The back side of the first leaf continues with the forty-nine-word paragraphs until we reach the twenty-eighth page (see page 120). The last numbered paragraph of forty-nine words is numbered 40 (remember the 41 in the square is crossed out).

But we need to fill forty-nine rows, and we only have forty paragraphs. How do we fill in the last nine rows of the back side of the first leaf table?

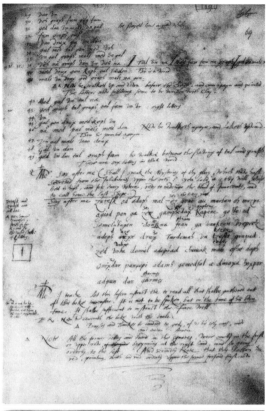

Paragraph 1
(49 words)

Figure A.2. Two pages from Dee's diary show the first and second of the forty-nine-word paragraphs for the front side of the first leaf, along with other marginal notes by Dee.

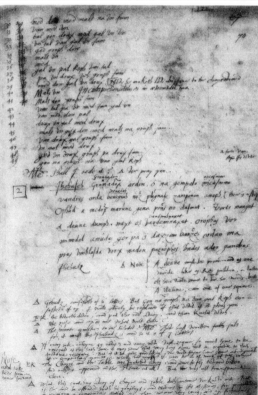

Paragraph 2
(49 words)

End of paragraph 49 from the front side of the first leaf table

Paragraph 2 is really the first row on the back side of the first leaf table)

Paragraph 3 (2nd row on back side)

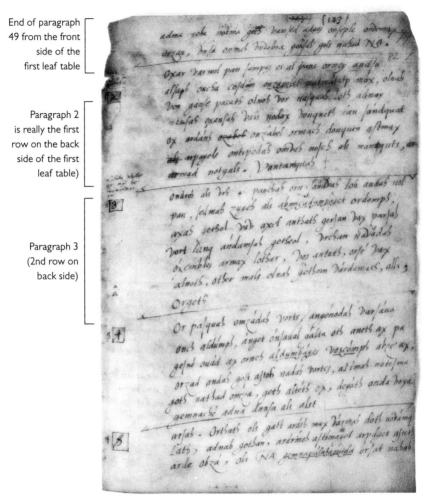

Figure A.3. Paragraphs on the back side of the first leaf containing forty-nine Enochian words transcribed by Dee.

Figure A.4 (at right and on page 120) shows the page with the fortieth paragraph of forty-nine words and a table consisting of nine rows and forty-nine columns filled in with letters, not words. This marks a transition, since up until now Enochian words were to be placed in each cell, but now only letters are to be used for the remaining table. These additional nine rows of letters complete the table of forty-nine rows and columns on the back side of the fist leaf. Thus the back side of the first leaf

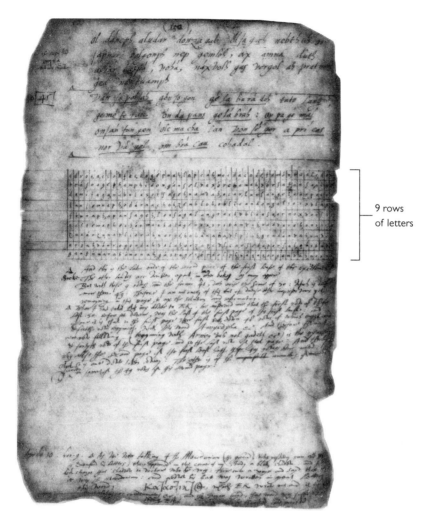

9 rows
of letters

Figure A.4. The nine rows and forty-nine columns
of letters that complete the back side of
the first leaf's forty-nine rows.

table is composed of forty rows of words and nine rows of letters. The
rest of the tables (2–48) are simply the forty-nine x forty-nine grid filled
in with letters, numbers, or left blank. Remember, each table that the
angels refer to is actually one leaf, with two sides—a front and a back.

The ninety-four tables, plus the two additional tables that are made
up of the pages of Enochian words in each cell, equal ninety-six pages

of tables. If we divide this by two, we get *forty-eight leaves*. This is consistent with the angel's statement that there are forty-eight tables or leaves.

To date, no one has been able to definitively decipher, interpret, or explain the meaning or use of these tables. This is the first time ever that the complete set of tables given to Dr. Dee by the angels has been printed in book form.

(**Note:** Both the front and back sides of the first leaf are located in MS Sloane 3188. Leaves 2 through 48 are in MS Sloane 3189. There is actually a duplicate set of the back side of the first leaf made by Kelly in MS Sloane 3189, but we have not included it here as it is not as clear and readable as the Dee copy.)

THE FIRST LEAF
OF THE BOOK OF ENOCH

From the diaries of Dr. John Dee,
written in his own hand

from the British Library MS Sloane 3188

The first leaf is comprised of twenty-eight pages of forty-nine paragraphs of Enochian words as well a small table of nine lines of forty-nine letters per line on the twenty-eighth page. The front side of the first leaf is shown in illustrations 1 through 20 on pages 92–112. The back side of the first leaf begins on page 112.

Dee included line numbers in the left margins to indicate each of the forty-nine-words paragraphs. Whenever a line or paragraph at the bottom of a page is carried over to the next page, I have included an a and b designation in the figure caption (e.g. line 5a, 5b, etc.).

Reminder: The first paragraph on the back side of the first leaf was incorrectly labeled 2 and is shown crossed out and correctly labeled 1 (see illustration 21 on page 113). Dee renumbered all the subsequent paragraphs to correctly identify the passages on the back side. So when we review the numbered paragraphs on the back side, we must not reference the numbers crossed out in the squares but the corrected numbers that appear to their left.

Previous
diary entries
that are not
part of the
first leaf

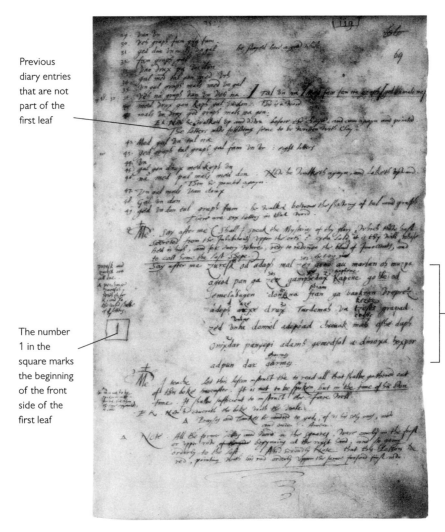

Paragraph
of 49 wo
is line I o
the first

The number
1 in the
square marks
the beginning
of the front
side of the
first leaf

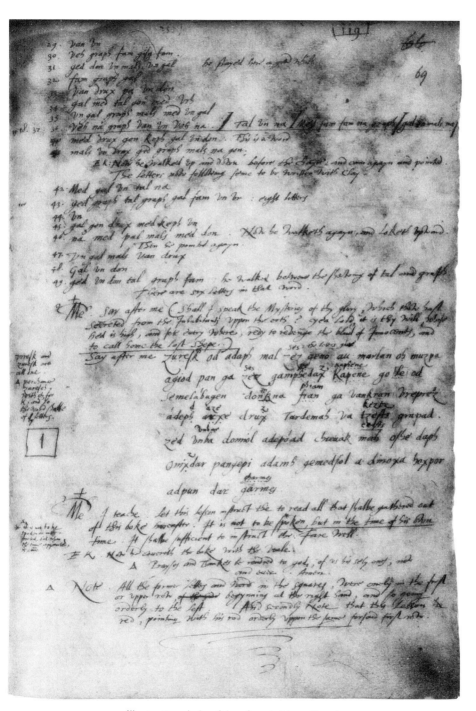

Illustration 1. Leaf 1 – front side – line 1

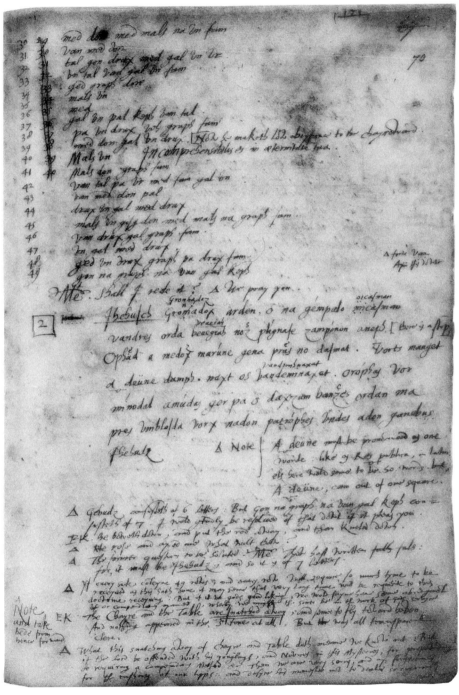

Illustration 2. Leaf 1 – front side – line 2

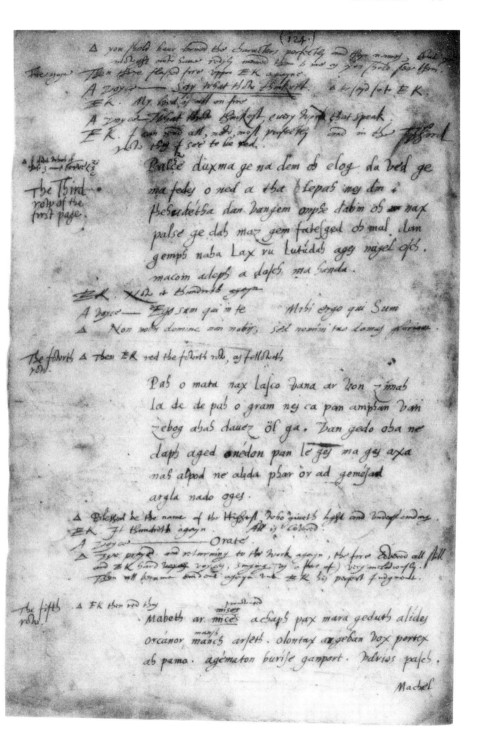

Illustration 3. Leaf 1 – front side – lines 3, 4, 5a

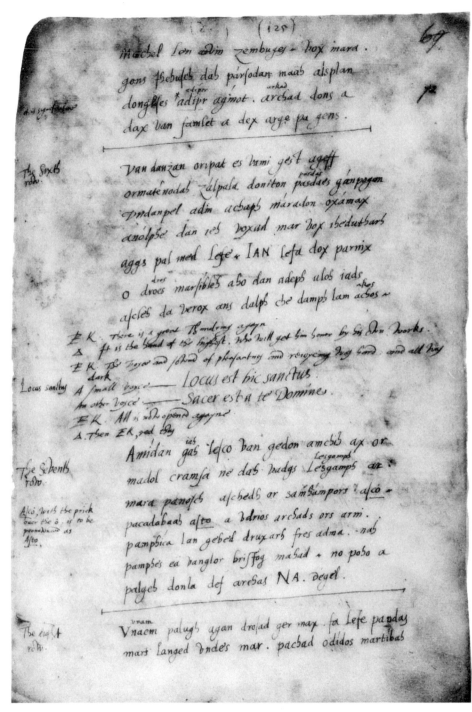

Illustration 4. Leaf I – front side – lines 5b, 6, 7, 8a

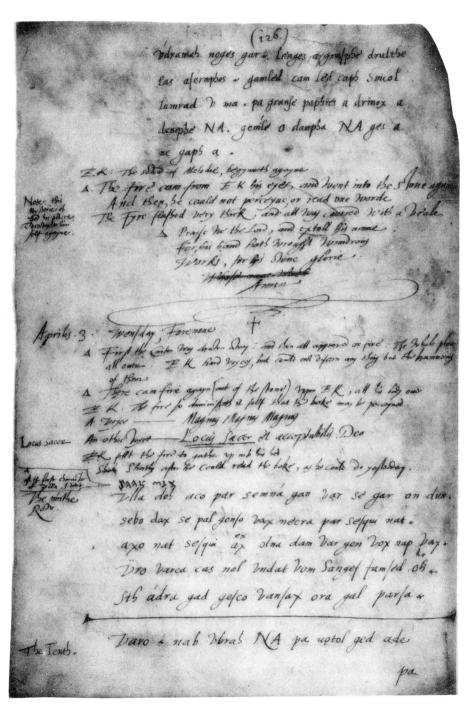

Illustration 5. Leaf I – front side – lines 8b, 9, 10a

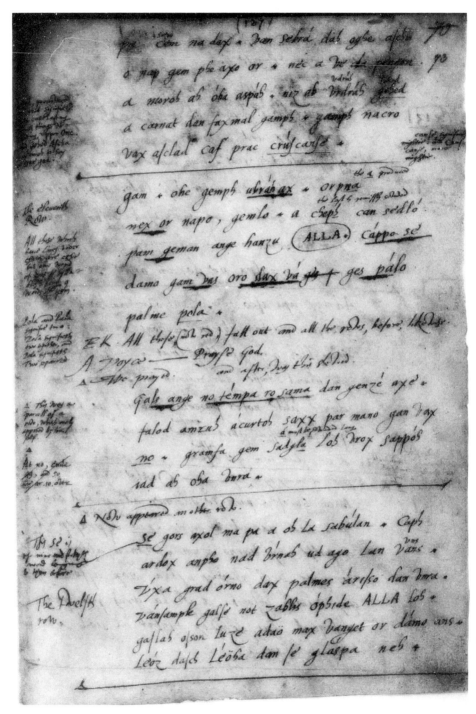

Illustration 6. Leaf 1 – front side – lines 10b, 11, 12

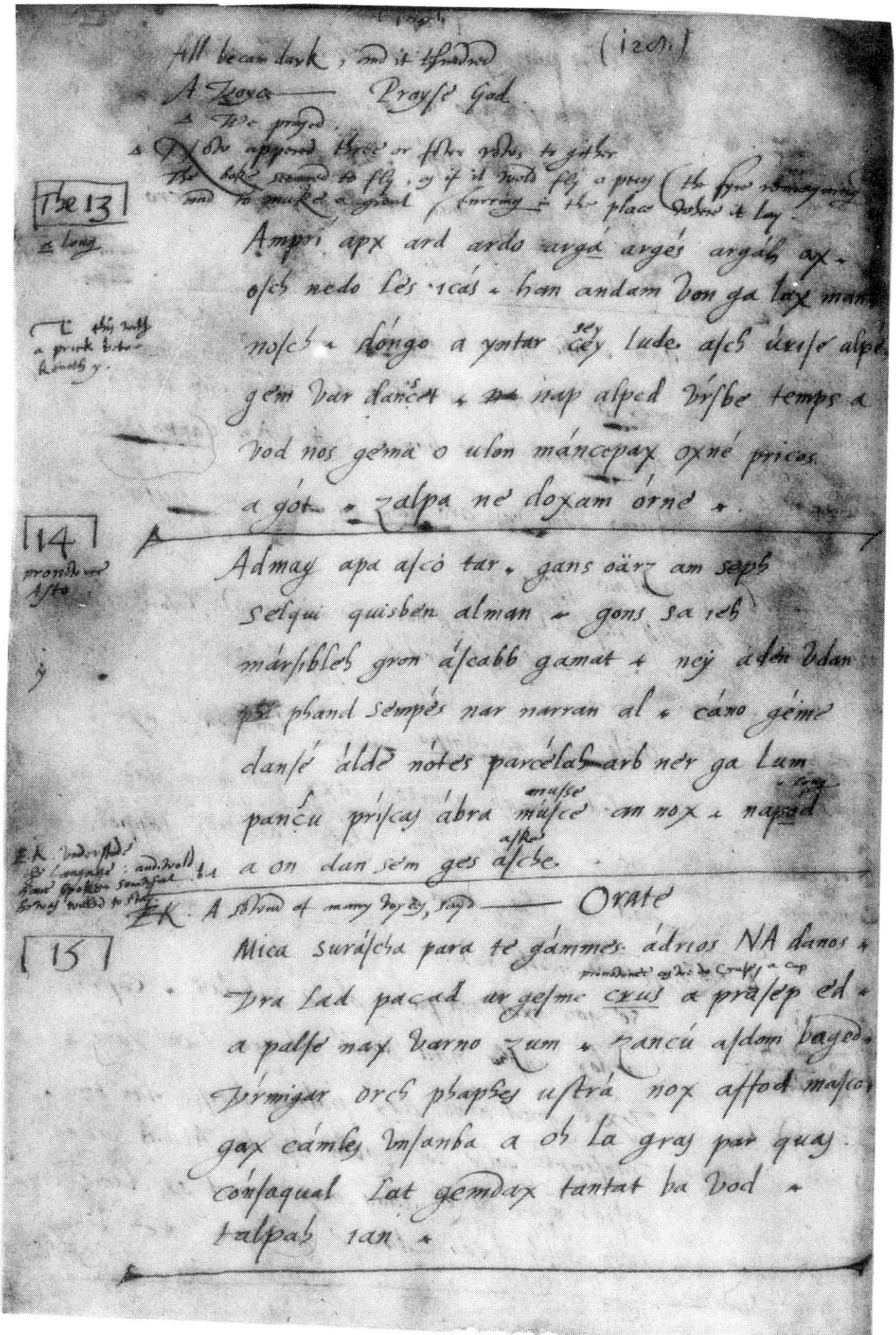
All becam dark, and it thundred (1201)
A Ileva —— Prayse God.
We prayed.
Ther appered three or fower rodes together
The boke seemed to fly, as if it wold fly a prey
and to make a great stirring in the place wher it lay.
The 13
Ampri apx ard ardo argá argés argáls ax.
ofcs nedo Lés icás. han andam Don ga lax man
nofcs. dongo a yntar cey lude afcs deife alp
gem Dar dancet. nap alped Drfbe temps a
Dod nos gemá o ulon mancepax oxné pricos
a gót. zalpa ne doxam orné.
14
Admay apa afcó tar. gans oärz am seps
selqui quisben alman. gons sa reb
mársibles gron áscabb gamat. nej aden Odan
phand sempés nar narran al. cáno geme
danfé áldé notés parcélab arb ner ga Lum
pancu priscay abra músce am nox. napad
a on dan sem ges afcbe.
EK. A sound of many voyces, sayd —— Orate
15
Mica surásca para te gámmes adrios NA danos.
Dra Lad pacad orgesme crus a prasep ed.
a palfe max Darno zum. zancú afdom baged.
Drmigar orcs phapses ustrá nox affod mascor
gax cámles Dnfanba a os La gras par quay.
consaqual Lat gemdax tantat ba Dod.
talpab ian.

Illustration 7. Leaf 1 – front side – lines 13, 14, 15

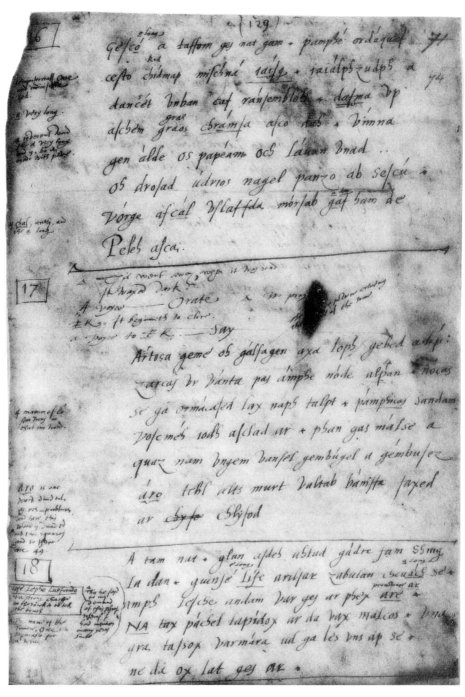

Illustration 8. Leaf 1 – front side – lines 16, 17, 18

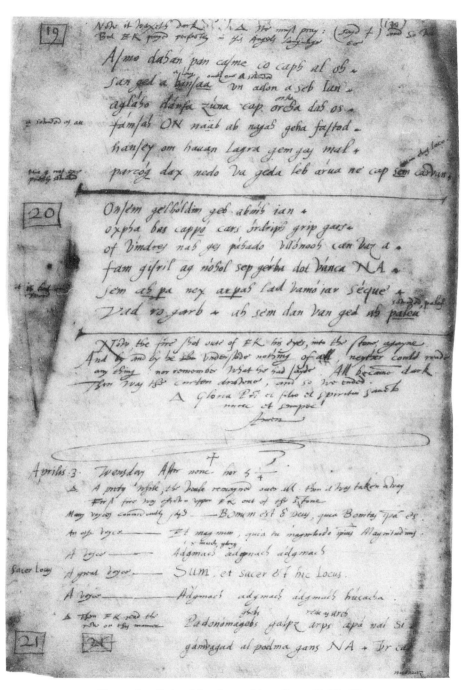

Illustration 9. Leaf 1 – front side – lines 19, 20, 21a

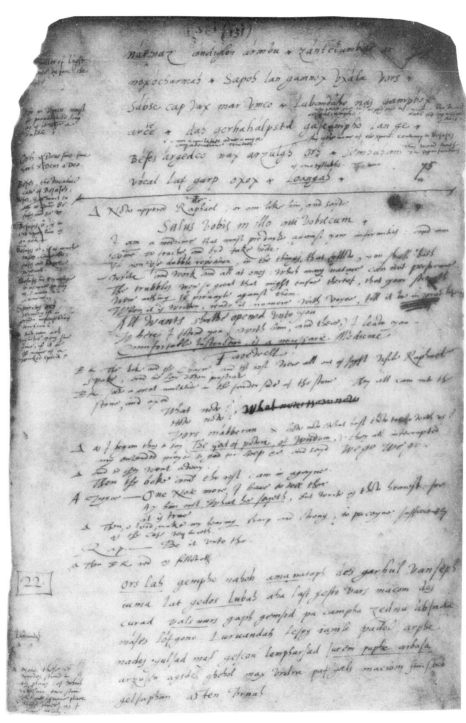

Illustration 10. Leaf 1 – front side – lines 21b, 22

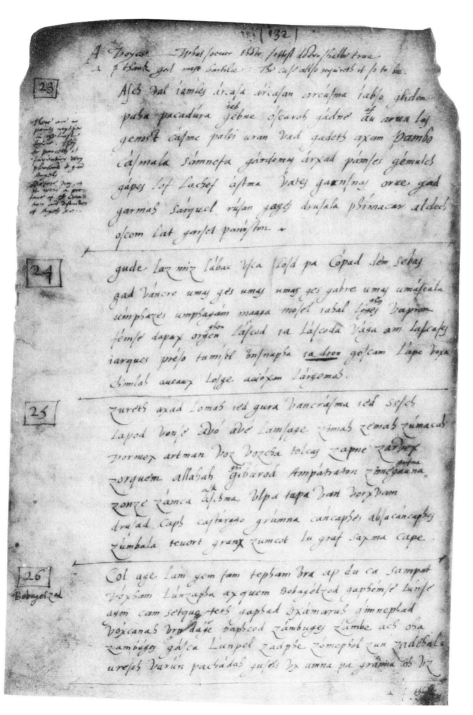

Illustration 11. Leaf 1 – front side – lines 23, 24, 25, 26

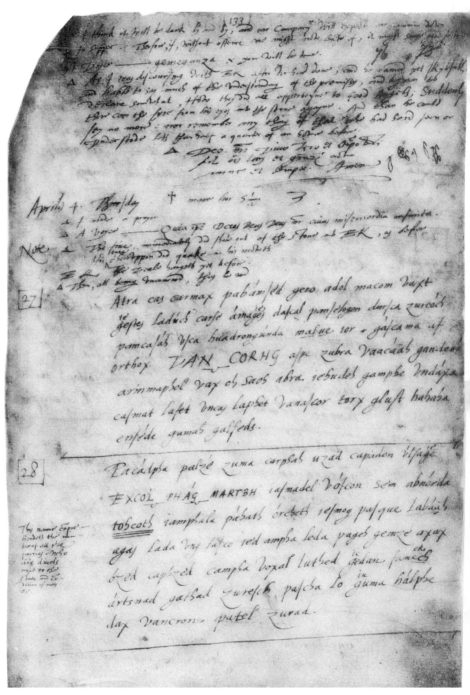

Illustration 12. Leaf 1 – front side – lines 27, 28

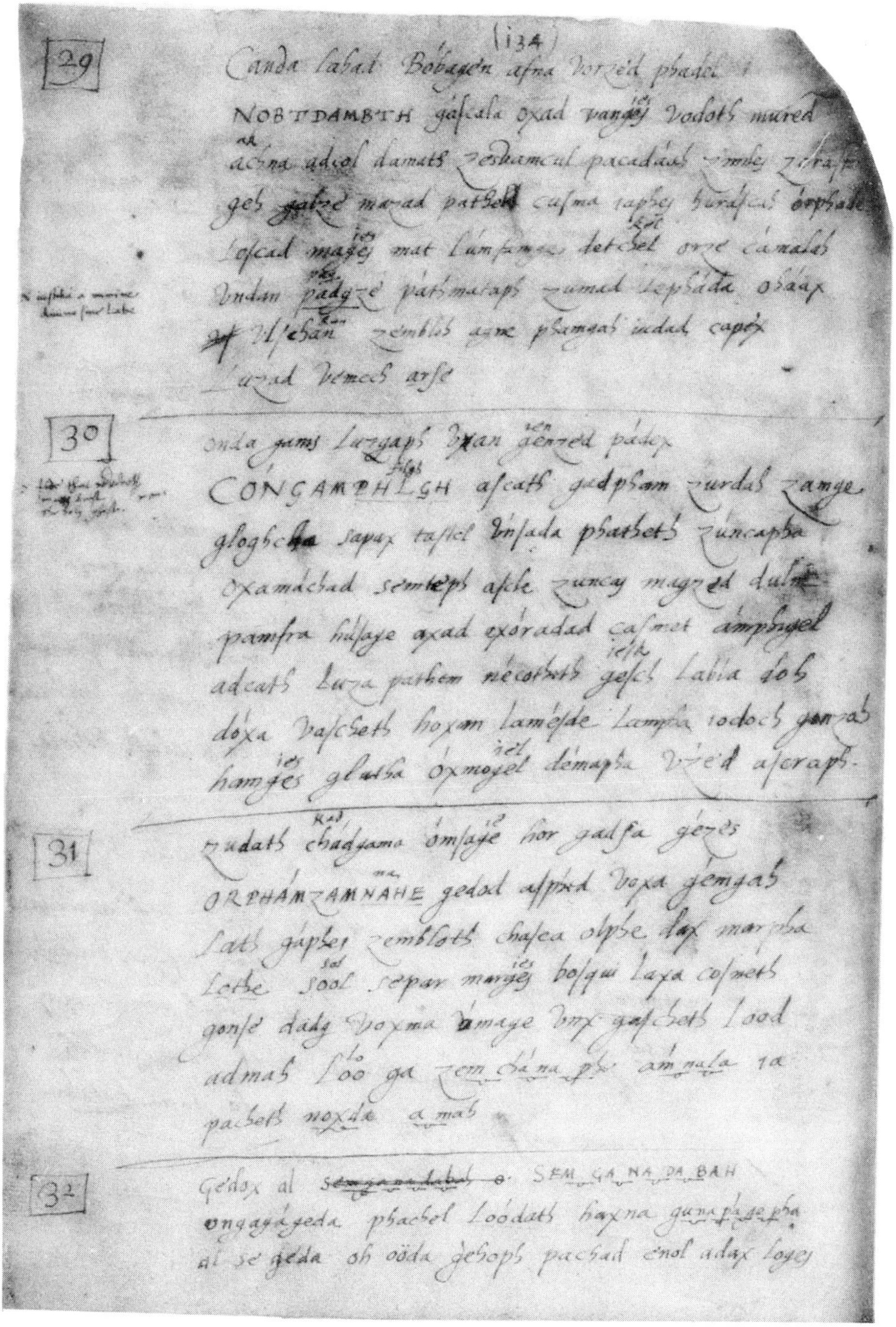

(134)

[29]

[30]

[31]

[32]

Illustration 13. Leaf 1 – front side – lines 29, 30, 31, 32a

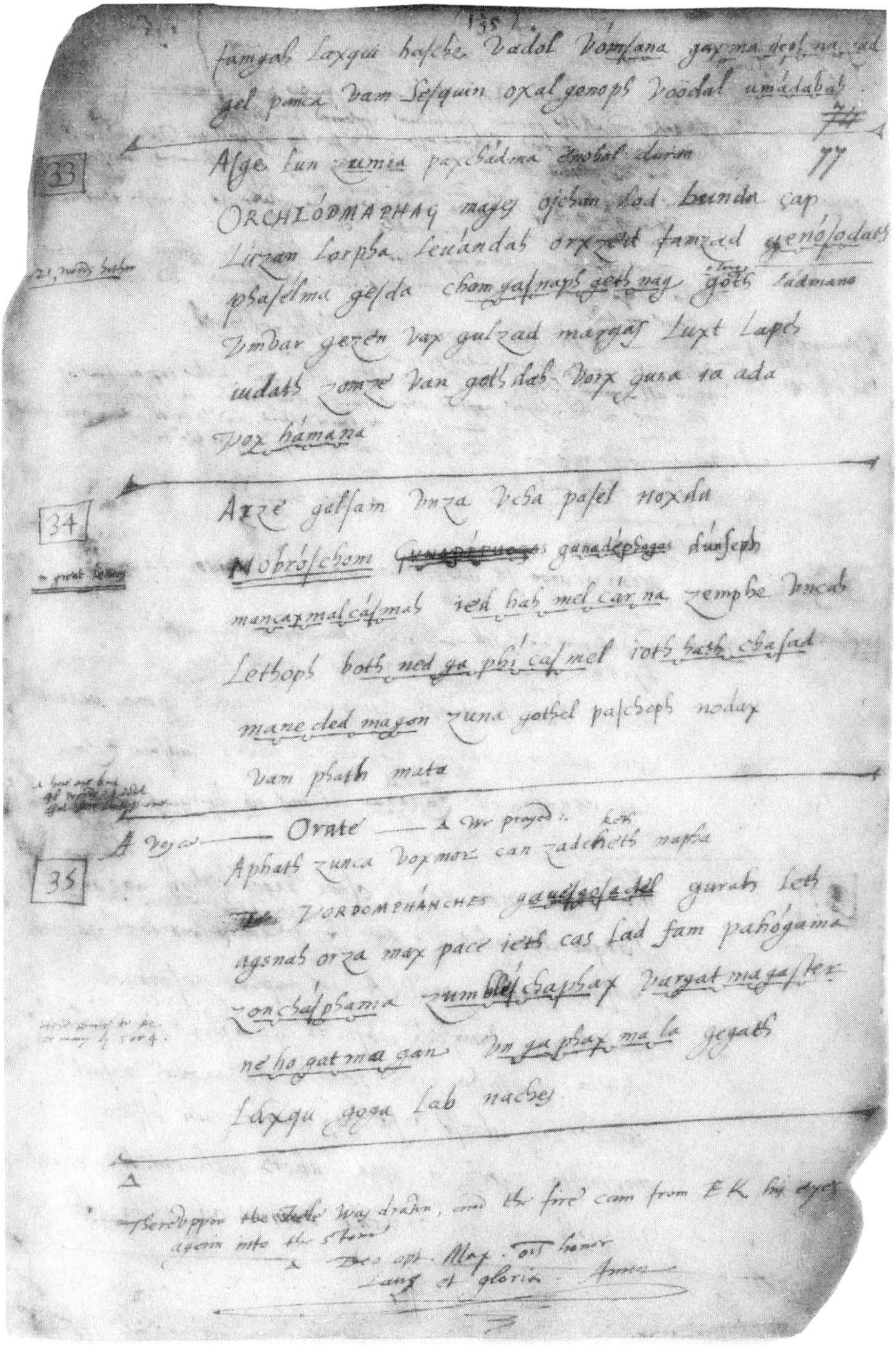

Illustration 14. Leaf 1 – front side – lines 32b, 33, 34, 35

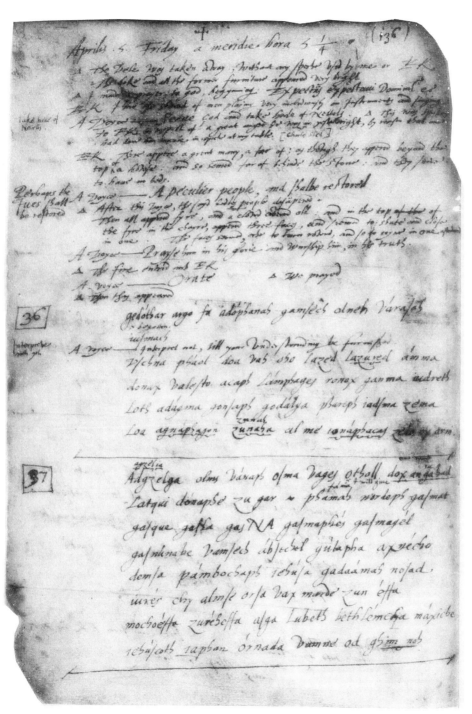

Illustration 15. Leaf 1 – front side – lines 36, 37

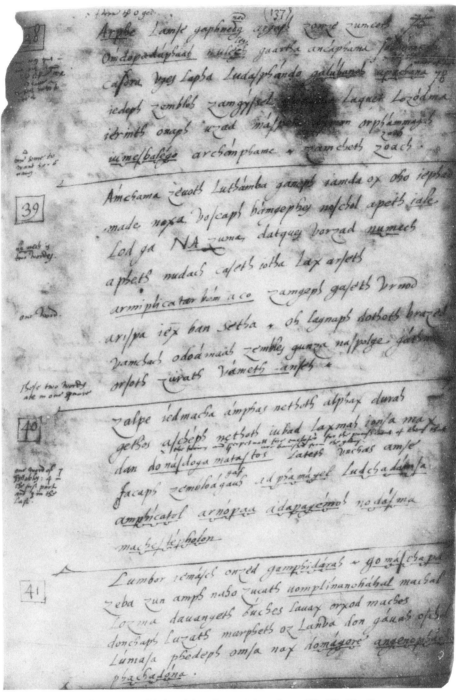

Illustration 16. Leaf 1 – front side – lines 38, 39, 40, 41

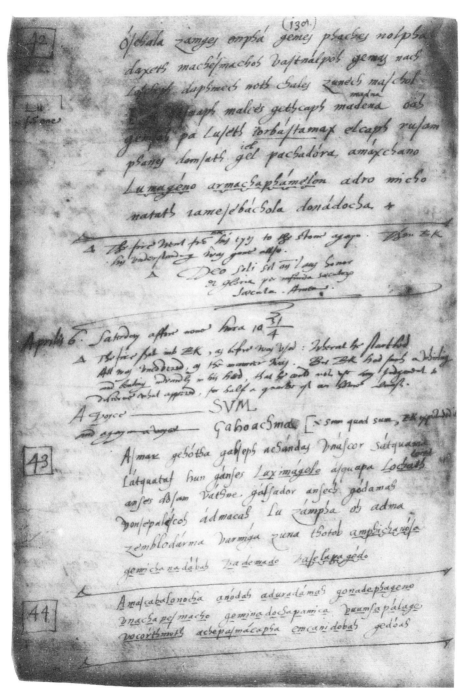

Illustration 17. Leaf 1 – front side – lines 42, 43, 44

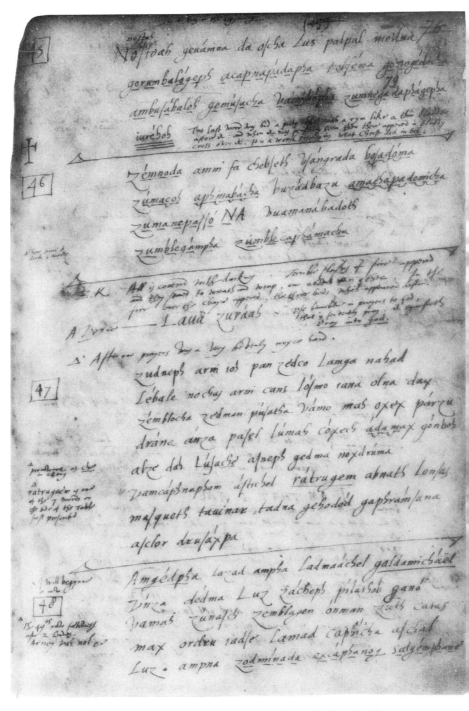

Illustration 18. Leaf 1 – front side – lines 45, 46, 47, 48a

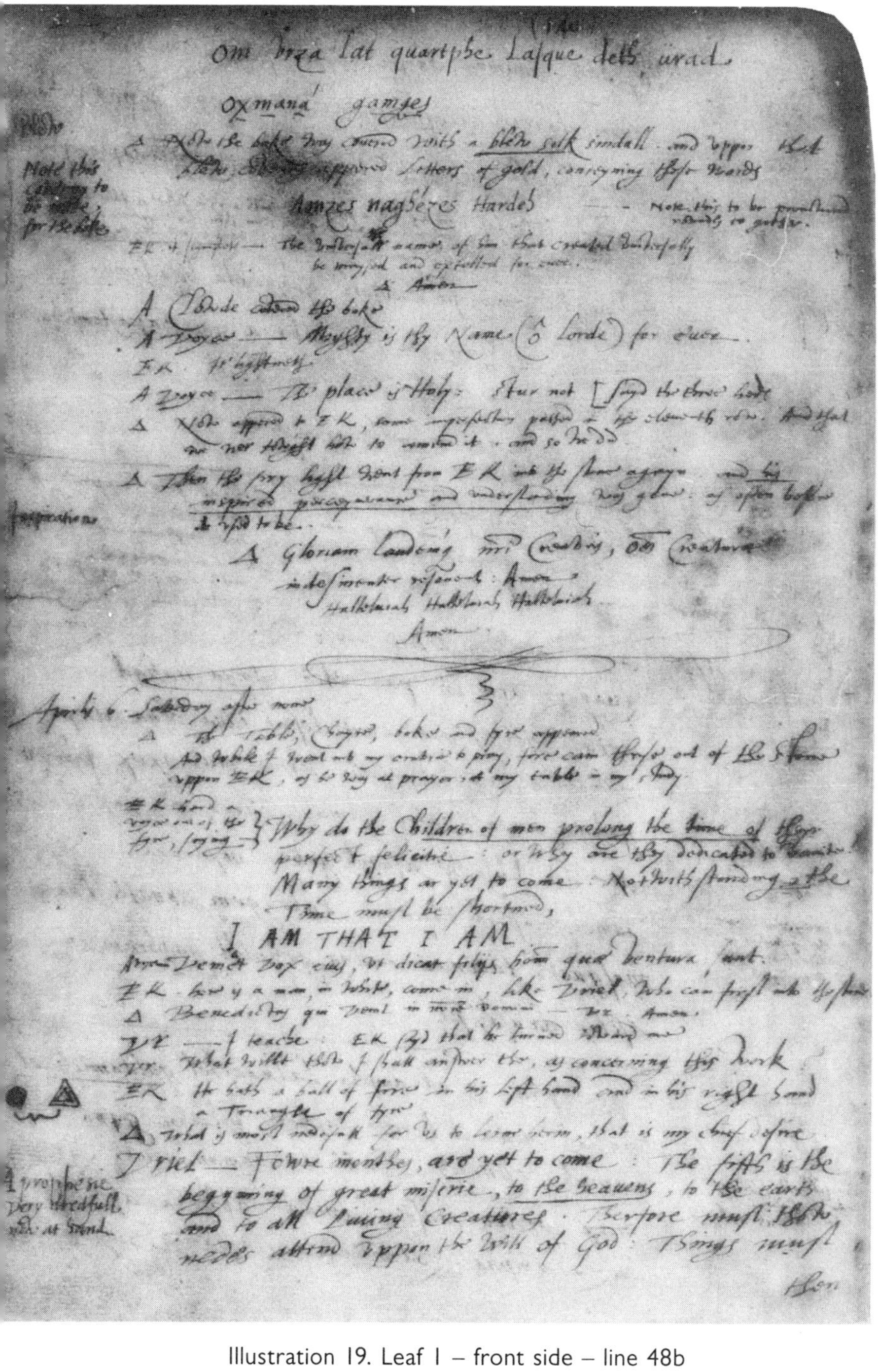

line 48b

Illustration 19. Leaf 1 – front side – line 48b

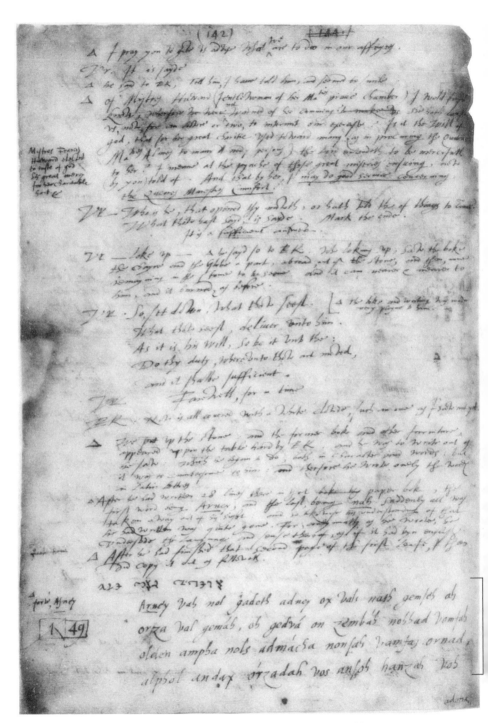

Illustration 20. Leaf I – front side – line 49a

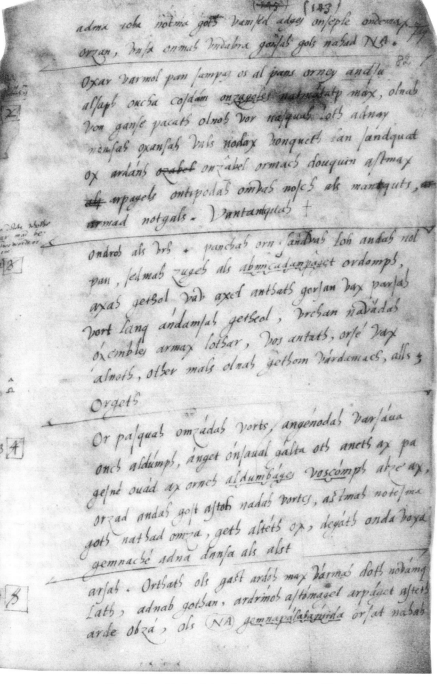

Illustration 21. Leaf 1 – front side – line 49b
and Leaf 1 – **back side** – lines 1–4a (incorrectly labeled 2–5 in figure)

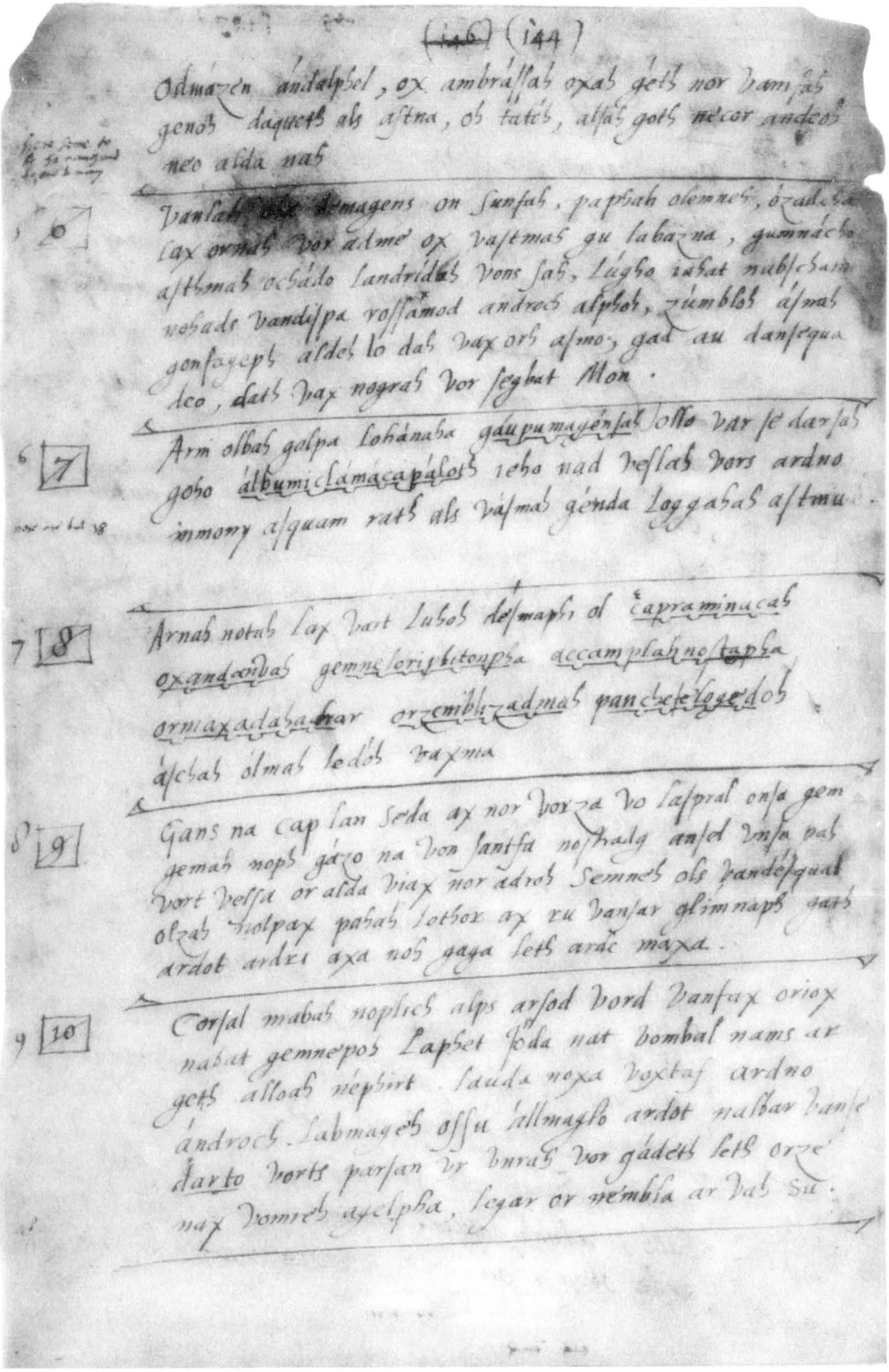
~~(146)~~ (144)

Odmazen andalpsel, ox ambrassas oxas gets nor vamsas
genos daquets als astma, os tates, alsas gots necor andeos
neo alda nas

6 Vanlas ... demagens on sansas, paphah olemnes, ozadesa
lax ormas vor adme ox vastmas gu labazna, gumnacho
asthmas ochado landridas vons sas, Lugho iahat nubsedam
vosads vandispa rossamod andros alphor, zumblas asmas
gonsayeps aldes lo das vax ors asmo, gad au dansequa
deo, dats vax nogras vor seghat Mon.

6 7 Arm olbas galpa Lohanaba gaupumagensal Josso var se darsas
goho albumiclamacapalos rebo nad vessas vors ardno
immomy asquam rats als vasmas genda Loggabas astmu.

7 8 Arnas notas lax vart lubos desmaphi ol capraminucas
oxandoonbas gemnelorishtonpsa accamplahnostapha
ormaxadabachar orzembluzadmas panchefelogedos
ascbas olmas ledos vaxma

8 9 Gans na cap lan seda ax nor vorza vo laspral onsa gem
gemas nops gazo na von santsa noshalg ansel vnsa vas
vort vessa or alda viax nor adros semnes ols vandesqual
olzas holpax pahas lothor ax ru vansar glimnaps gars
ardot ardri axa nos gaga lets arac maxa.

9 10 Corsal mabas noplics alps arsod vord vansax oriox
nabat gemnepos Lapset soda nat vombal nams ar
gets alloas nepsirt sauda noxa voxtas ardno
androcs labmages ossu allmaglo ardot nalbar vanse
darto vorts parsan vr vnras vor gadets lets orze
nax vomres ayelpha, segar or nembla ar vas su.

Illustration 22. Leaf 1 – back side – lines 4b–9 (labeled 5–10 in figure)

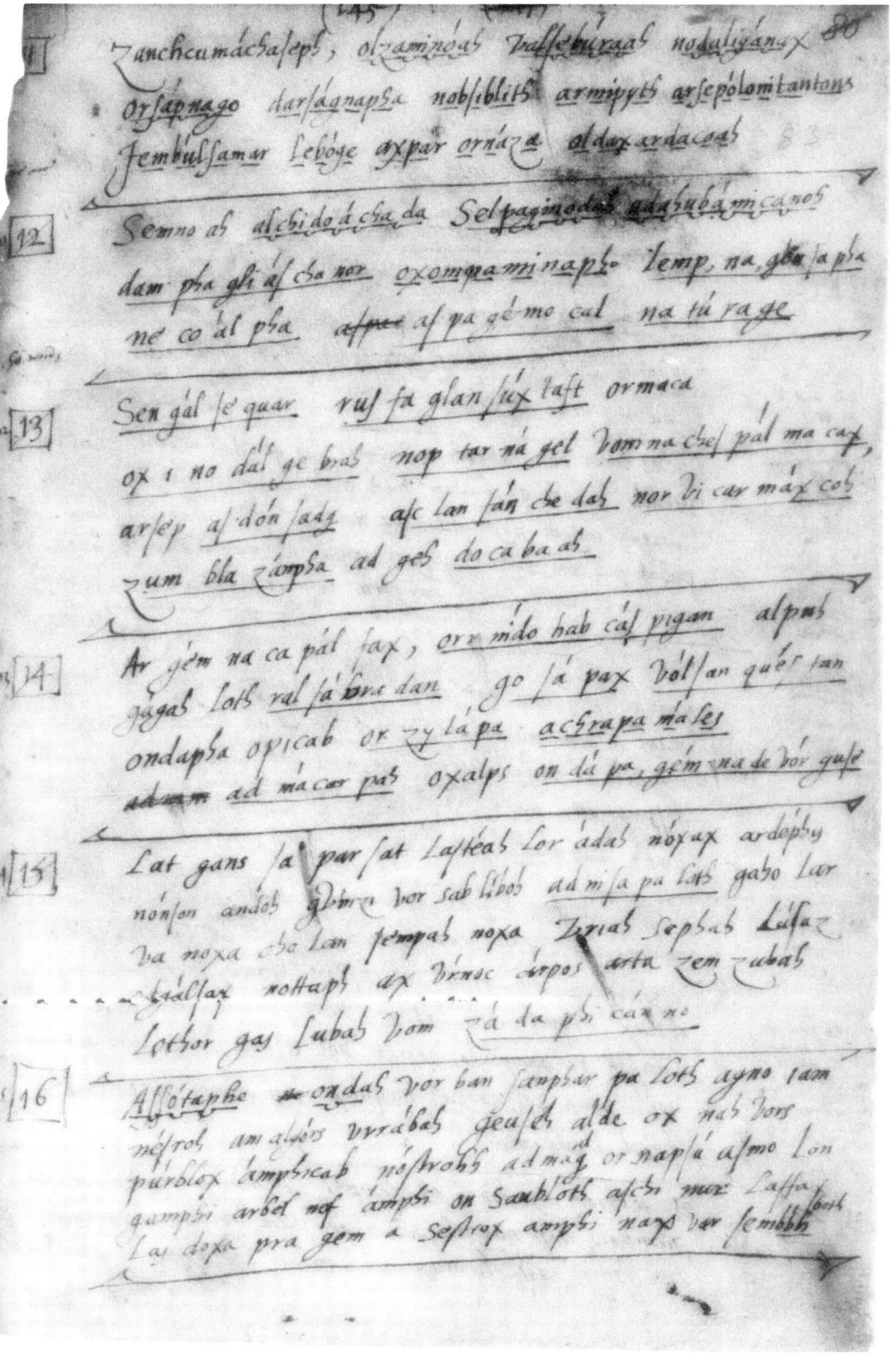

Illustration 23. Leaf 1 – back side – lines 10–15 (labeled 11–16 in figure)

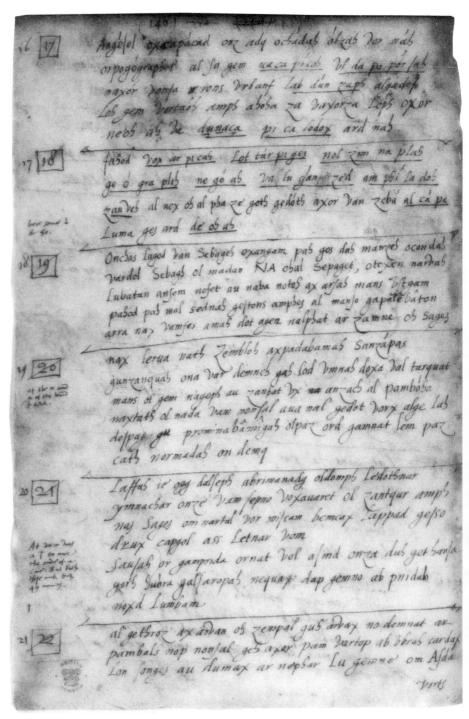

Illustration 24. Leaf 1 – back side – lines 16–21a (labeled 17–22 in figure)

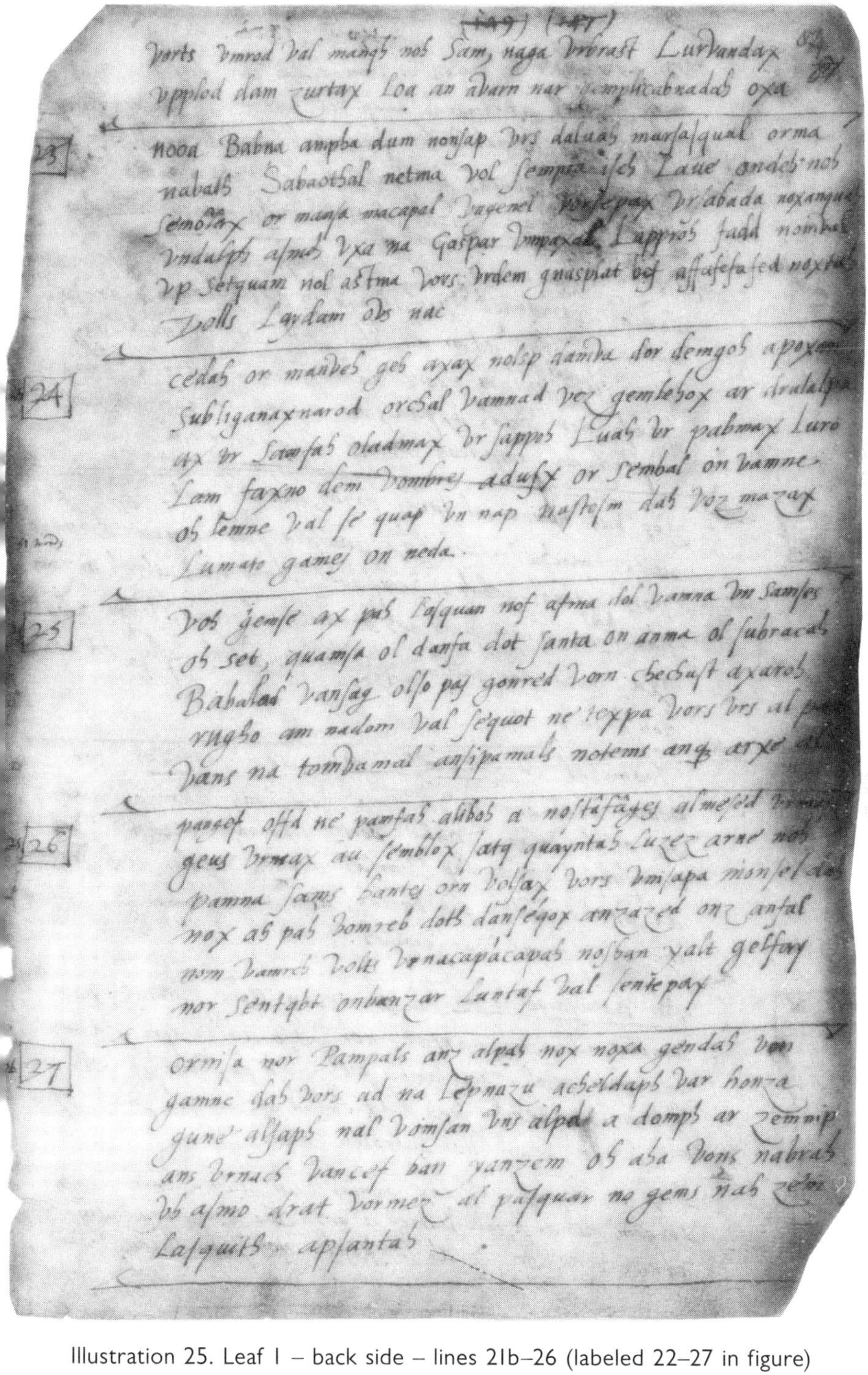
Vorts vmrod val mangs nos Sam, naga vrbrast Lurvandax
vpplod dam zurtax Loa an abarn nar zemplicabradabs oxa
23 nooa Babna ampha dum nonsap vrs daluas marsasqual orma
nabats Sabaotsal netma vol sempra isbs Laue ondebnos
semodax or mansa macapal vagenel vonsepax vr abada noxamque
vndalpbs asmos vxa na Gaspar vmpaxab Lappros sadd nombax
vp Setquam nol astma vors vrdem quasplat vos affafefafed noxtal
Volls Lardam ods nac
24 cedabs or mandes ges axax nolsp damda dor demgos apoxam
Subliganaxnarod orcsal vamnad vez gemlesox ar dradalpa
ax vr Sawfas oladmax vr sappos Luab vr pabmax Luro
Lam faxno dem vombres adusx or sembal on vamne
os temne val se quap vn nap mastosm dab voz mazax
Lamato games on neda
25 Vos gemse ax pas sasquan nos asma dol vamna vm Sanses
os set, quamsa ol dansa dot santa on anma ol subracab
Babalad vansag olso pas gonred vorn chesust axarob
vngbo am nadom val sequot ne toxpa vors vrs al pa
vans na tomdamal ansipamals notems angs arxe
26 pasnef osd ne pamfas alibos a nostafagsi almesed vrmes
geus vrmax au semblox satq quayntab Luzez arne nos
pamna sams santes orn vossax vors vmsapa monsel das
nox as pas vomreb dots dansegox anzazed onz ansal
nom vamres volts vrnacapacapas nosban yalt gelfary
nor sentqbt onbanzar Lantaf val seniepax
27 ormisa nor Pampals anz alpas nox noxa gendas vom
gamne dab vors ad na Lepnazu acseldaps var honza
gune alsaps nal vomsan vns alpas a domps ar zemmip
ans vrnacs vancef ban yanzem os asa vons nabras
vs asmo drat vormez al pasquar no gems nab zelon
Lasquits apsantas

Illustration 25. Leaf I – back side – lines 21b–26 (labeled 22–27 in figure)

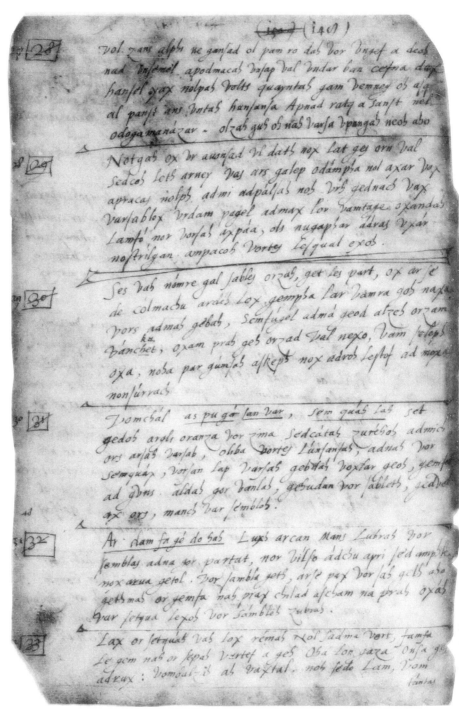

Illustration 26. Leaf I – back side – lines 27–32a (labeled 28–33 in figure)

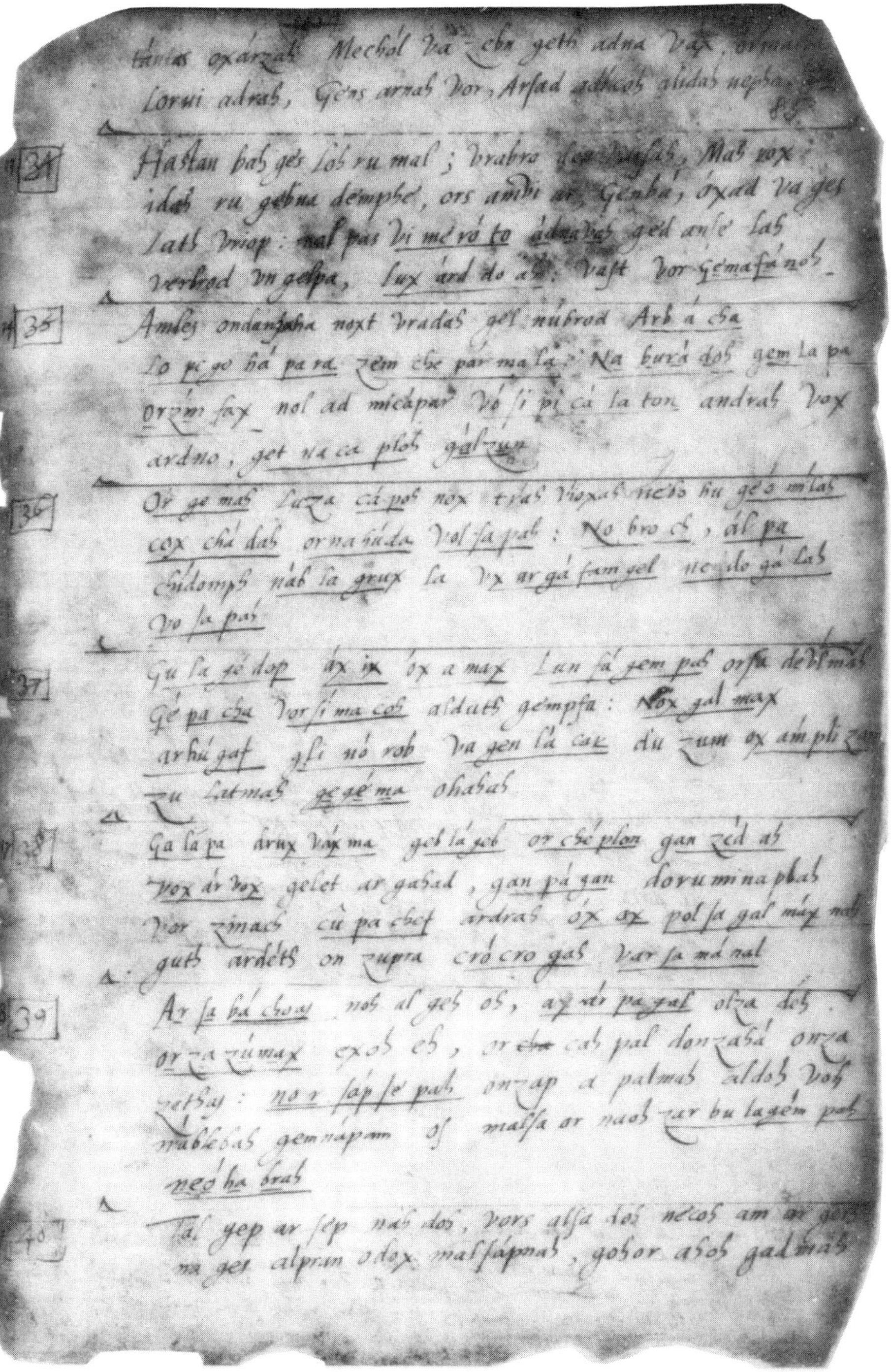

Illustration 27. Leaf I – back side – lines 32b–39a (labeled 33–40 in figure)

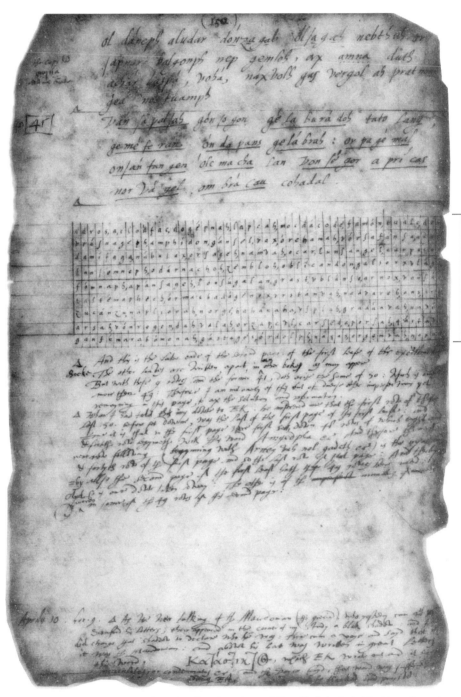

Illustration 28. Leaf I – back side – lines 39b–40 (labeled 40–41 in figure)
and the nine lines of the small table (lines 41–49).

THE FORTY-SEVEN TABLES

Leaf 2 (Table 2) to Leaf 48 (Table 48)

As transcribd by Edward Kelley

Ninety-four pages of individual tables
from the British Library MS Sloane 3189

In the previous pages we reproduced both the front and back
sides of leaf 1. The next section has both the front and
back sides of each of the remaining 47 leaves (leaves 2–48),
thus completing the 48 Tables that the angels gave to Dee and
Kelley. These tables (2–48) are all in Kelley's handwriting, and
no one to this day has been able to interpret or understand
these tables. I do not believe that even Kelley or Dr. Dee knew
what they meant or how to interpret them but left them for
some future time to decode.

Table 2

Leaf 2 – front side

Table 2

Leaf 2 – back side

Table 3

Leaf 3 – front side

Table3

Leaf 3 – back side

Table 4

Leaf 4 – front side

Table 4

Leaf 4 – back side

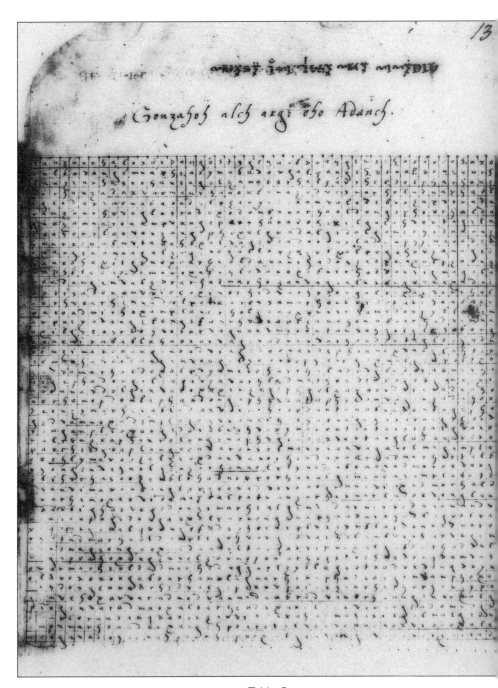

Table 5

Leaf 5 – front side

Table 5

Leaf 5 – back side

Table 6

Leaf 6 – front side

Table 6

Leaf 6 — back side

Table 7

Leaf 7 – front side

Table 7

Leaf 7 — back side

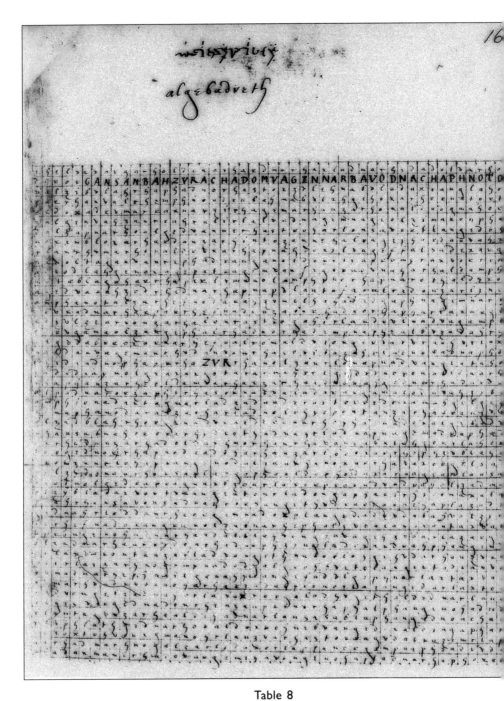

Table 8

Leaf 8 – front side

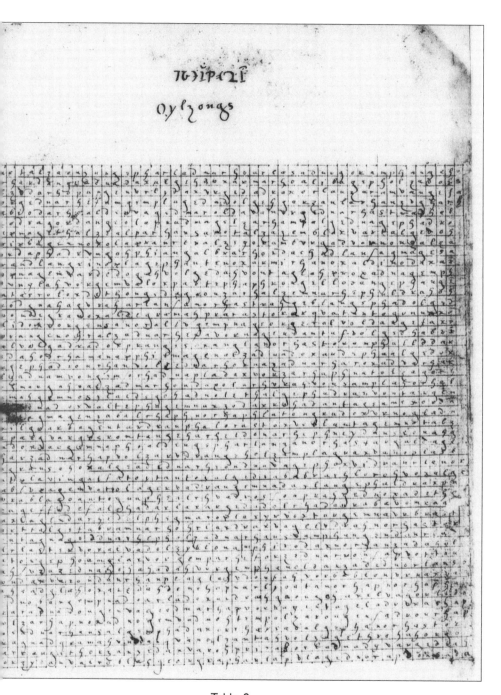

Table 8

Leaf 8 – back side

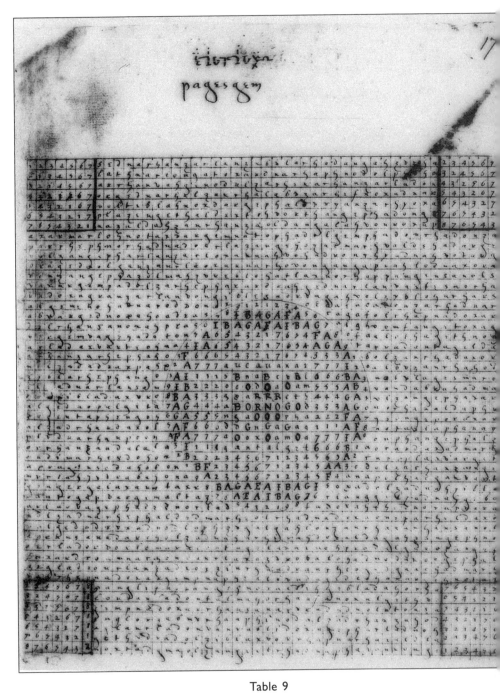

Table 9

Leaf 9 – front side

Table 9

Leaf 9 – back side

Table 10

Leaf 10 – front side

Table 10

Leaf 10 – back side

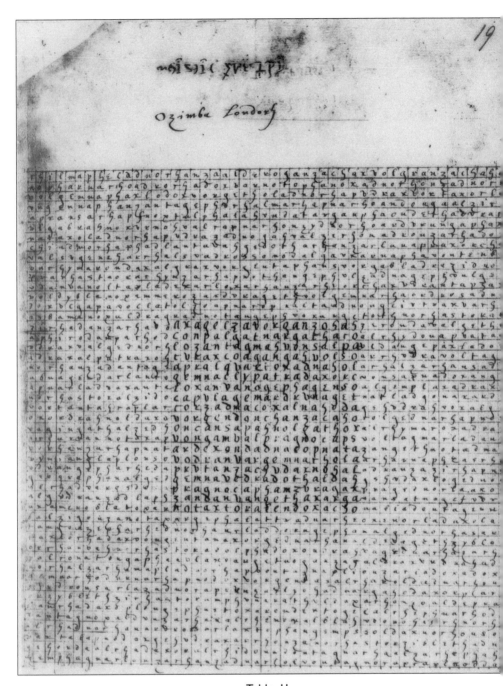

Table 11

Leaf 11 – front side

Table II

Leaf II – back side

Table 12

Leaf 12 – front side

Table 12

Leaf 12 – back side

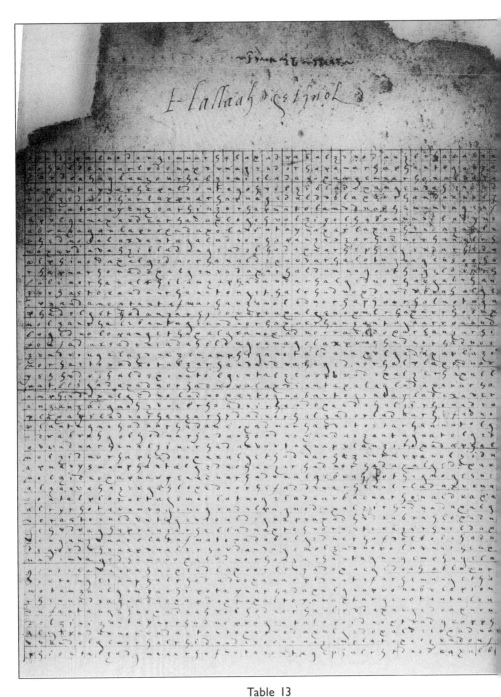

Table 13

Leaf 13 – front side

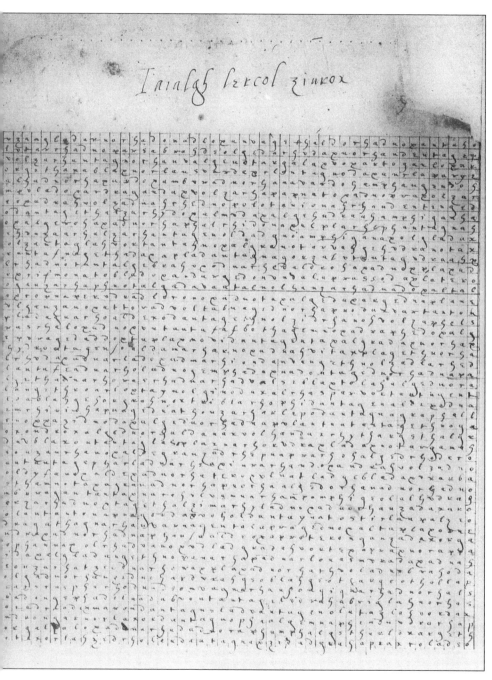

Table 13

Leaf 13 – back side

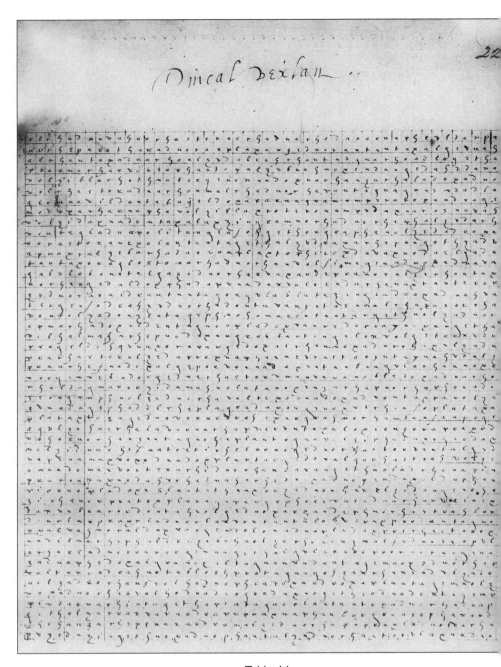

Table 14

Leaf 14 – front side

Table 14

Leaf 14 – back side

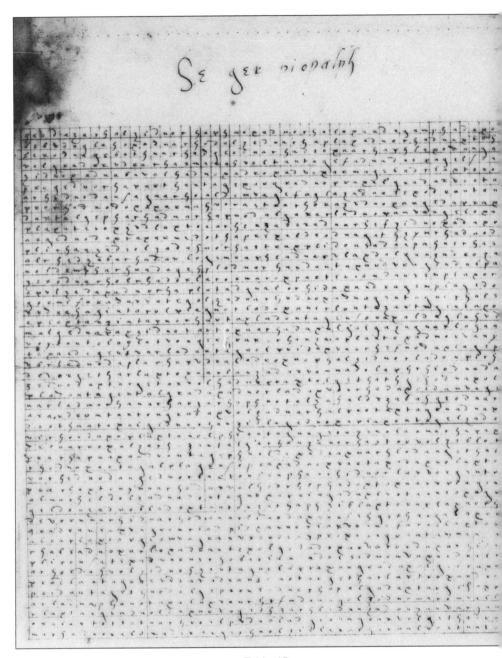

Table 15

Leaf 15 – front side

Table 15

Leaf 15 – back side

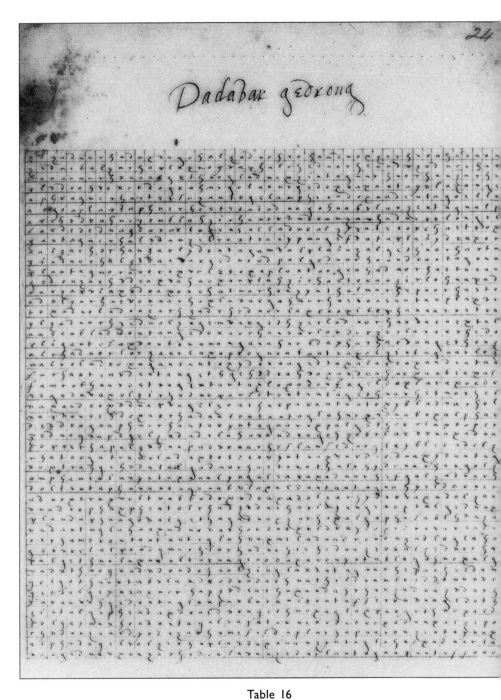

Table 16

Leaf 16 — front side

Table 16

Leaf 16 – back side

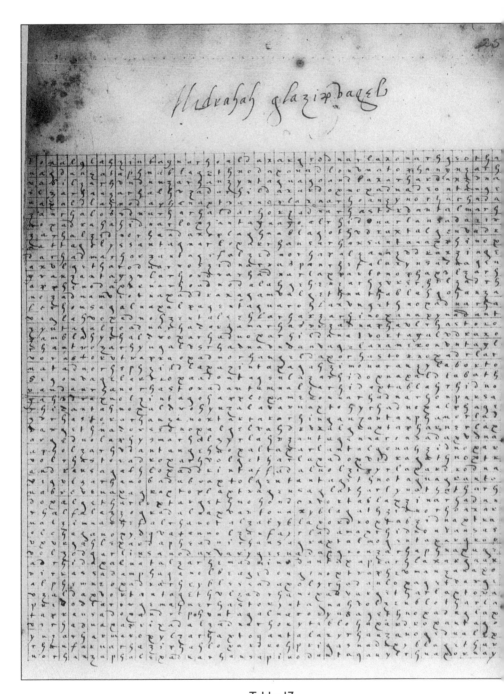

Table 17

Leaf 17 – front side

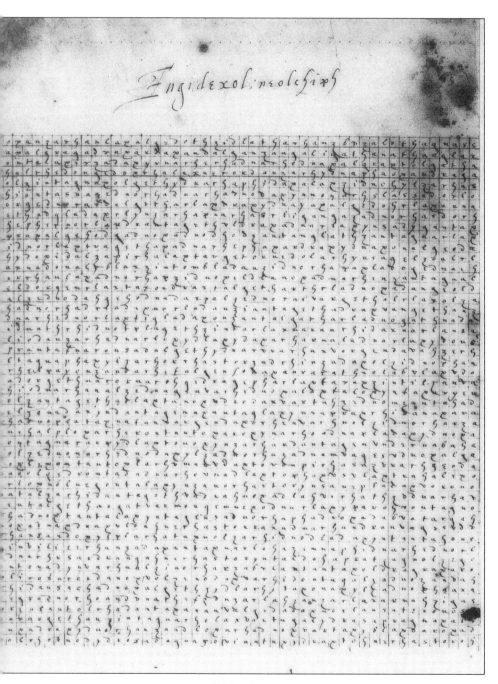

Table 17

Leaf 17 – back side

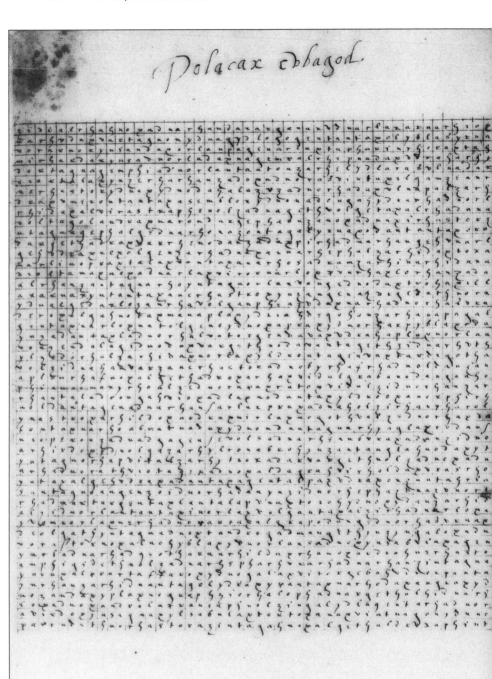

Table 18

Leaf 18 – front side

Table 18

Leaf 18 – back side

Table 19

Leaf 19 – front side

Table 19

Leaf 19 – back side

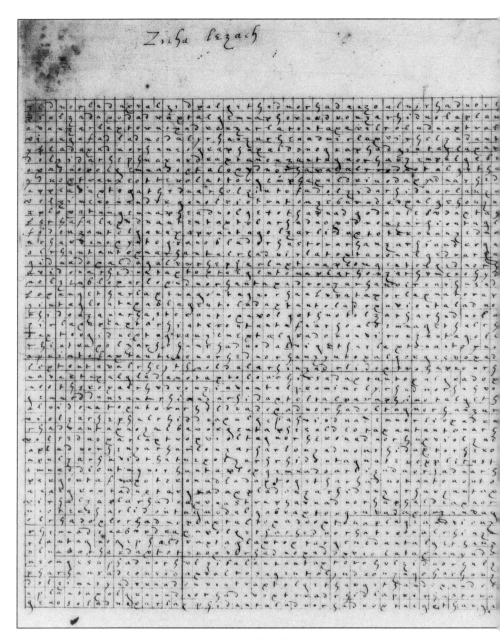

Table 20

Leaf 20 – front side

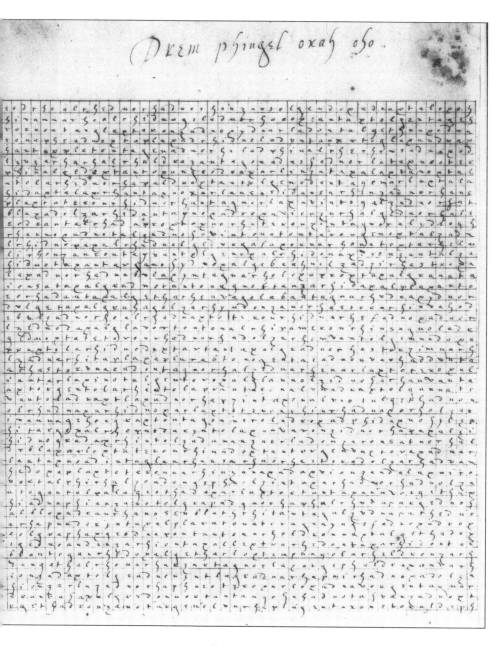

Table 20

Leaf 20 – back side

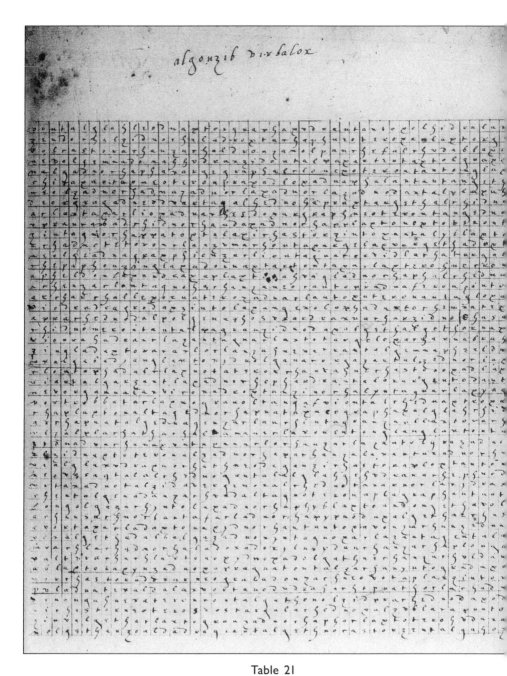

Table 21

Leaf 21 – front side

Table 21

Leaf 21 — back side

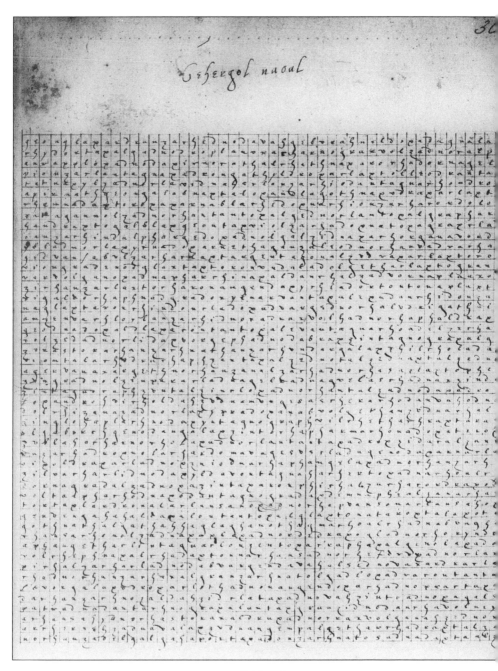

Table 22

Leaf 22 – front side

Table 22

Leaf 22 – back side

Table 23

Leaf 23 – front side

Table 23

Leaf 23 – back side

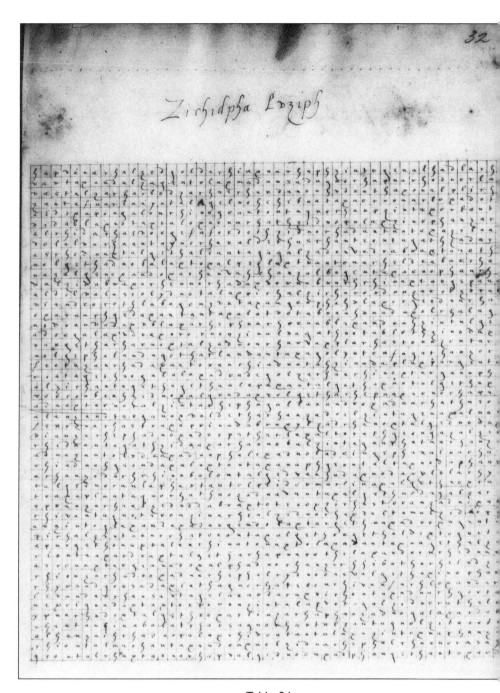

Table 24

Leaf 24 – front side

Table 24

Leaf 24 – back side

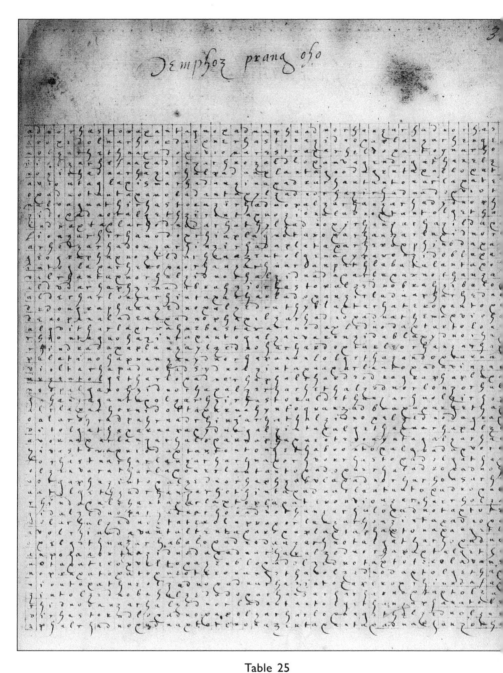

Table 25

Leaf 25 – front side

Table 25
Leaf 25 — back side

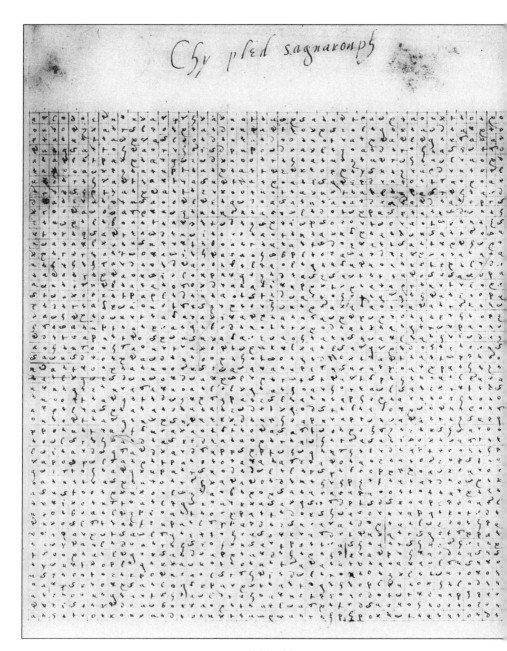

Table 26

Leaf 26 – front side

Table 26

Leaf 26 – back side

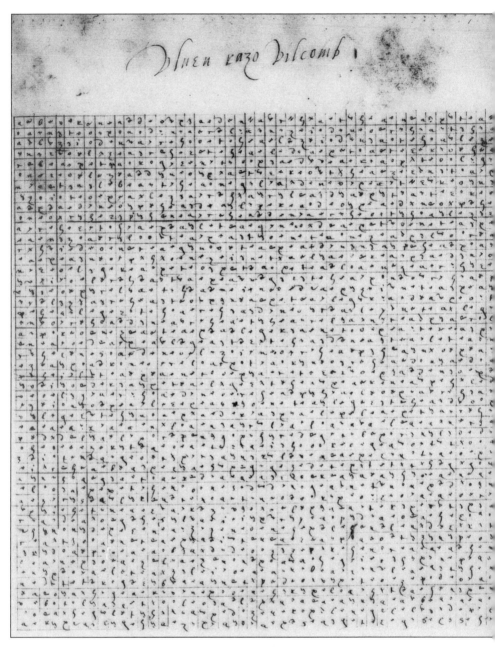

Table 27

Leaf 27 – front side

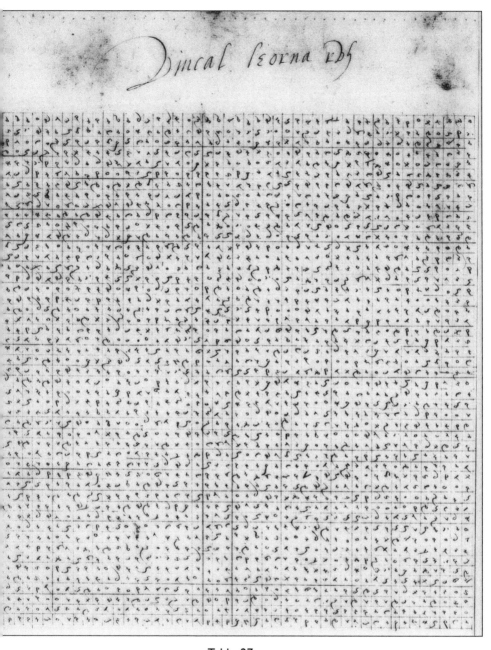

Table 27

Leaf 27 – back side

Table 28

Leaf 28 – front side

Table 28

Leaf 28 – back side

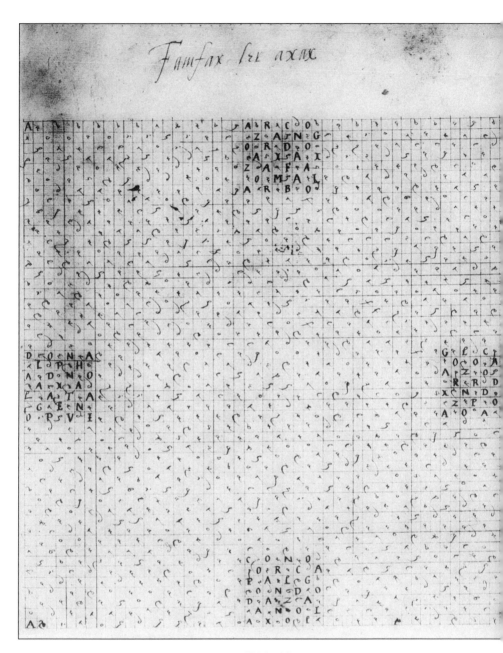

Table 29

Leaf 29 – front side

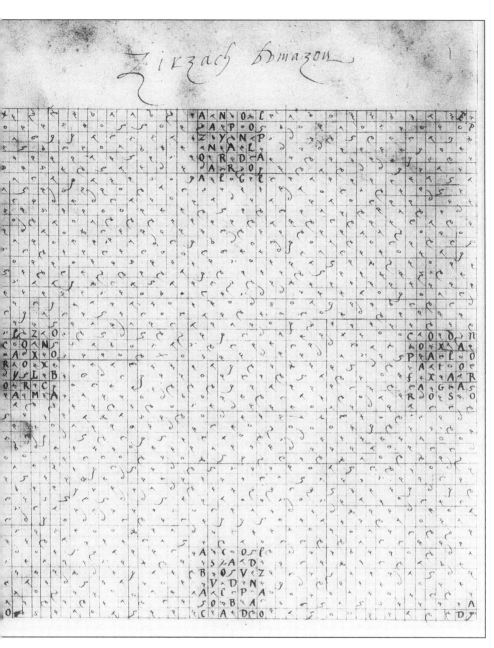

Table 29

Leaf 29 – back side

Table 30

Leaf 30 – front side

Table 30

Leaf 30 – back side

Table 31

Leaf 31 – front side

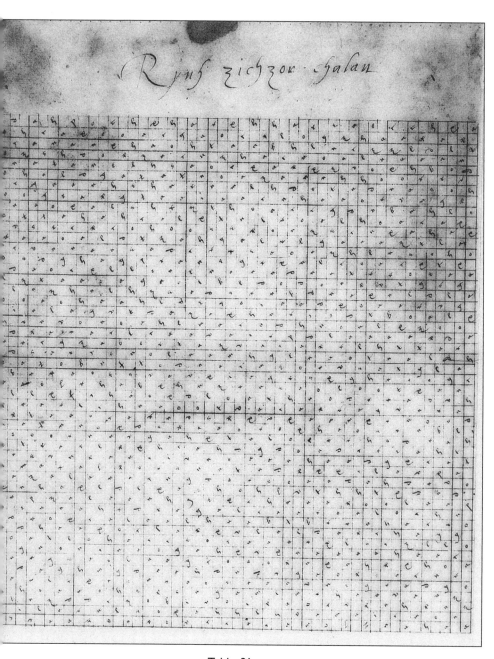

Table 31

Leaf 31 – back side

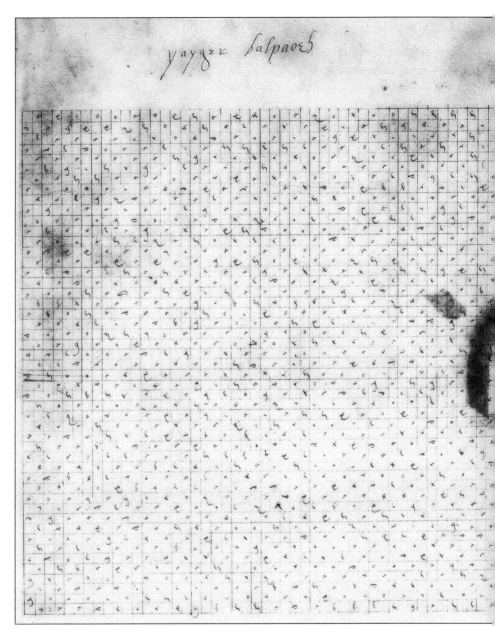

Table 32

Leaf 32 – front side

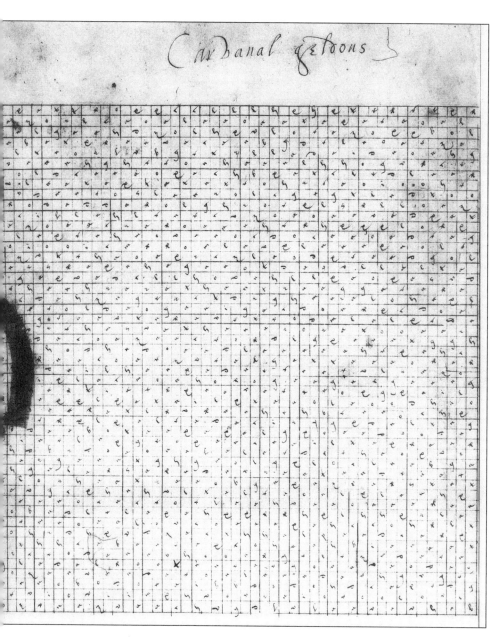

Table 32

Leaf 32 – back side

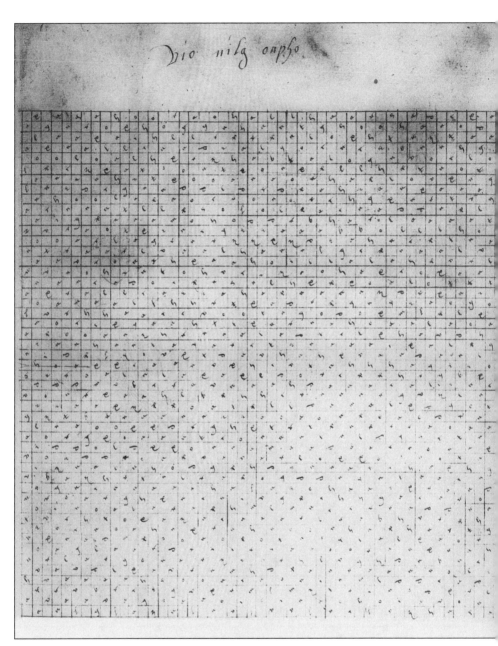

Table 33

Leaf 33 – front side

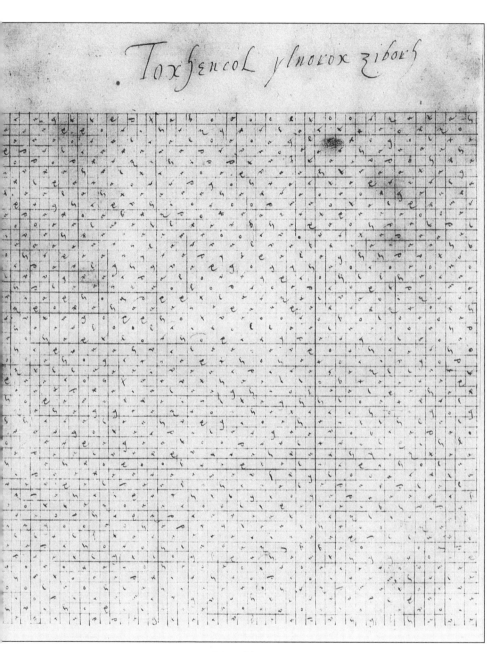

Table 33

Leaf 33 – back side

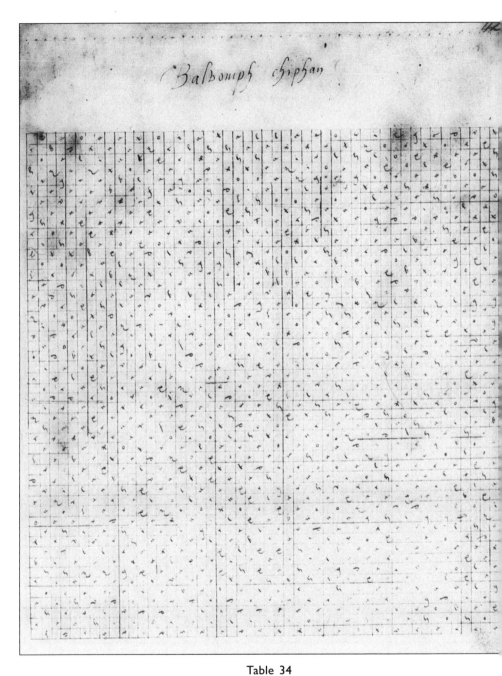

Table 34

Leaf 34 – front side

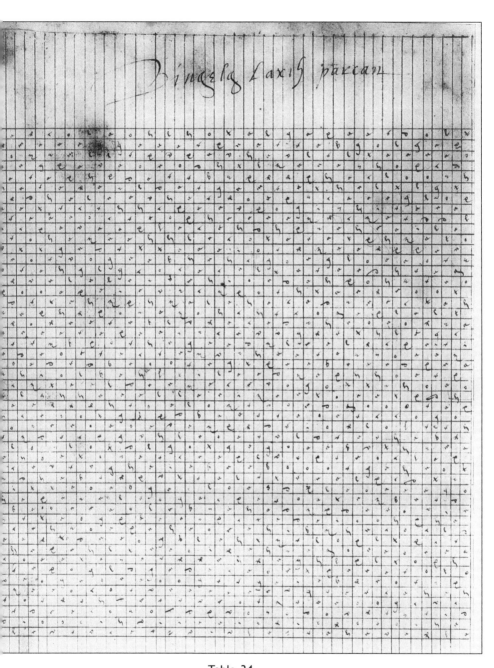

Table 34

Leaf 34 – back side

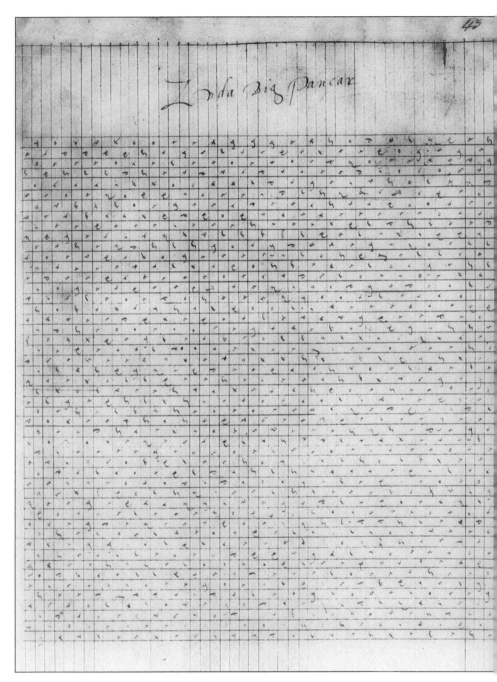

Table 35

Leaf 35 – front side

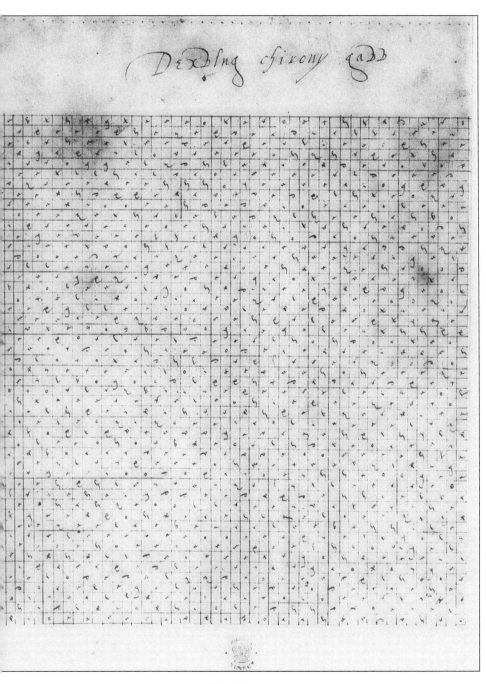

Table 35

Leaf 35 – back side

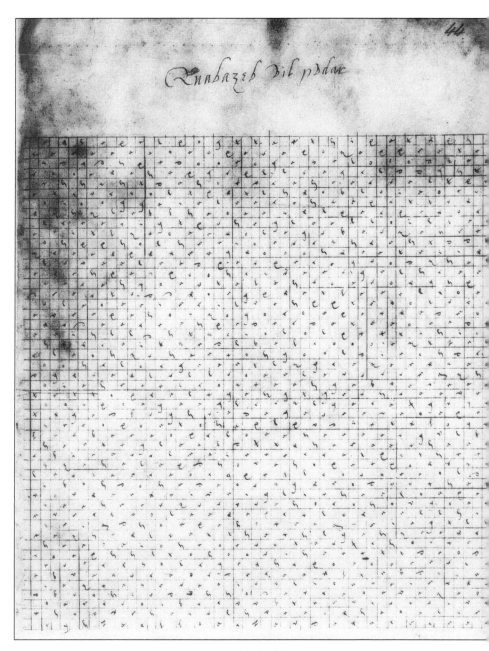

Table 36

Leaf 36 – front side

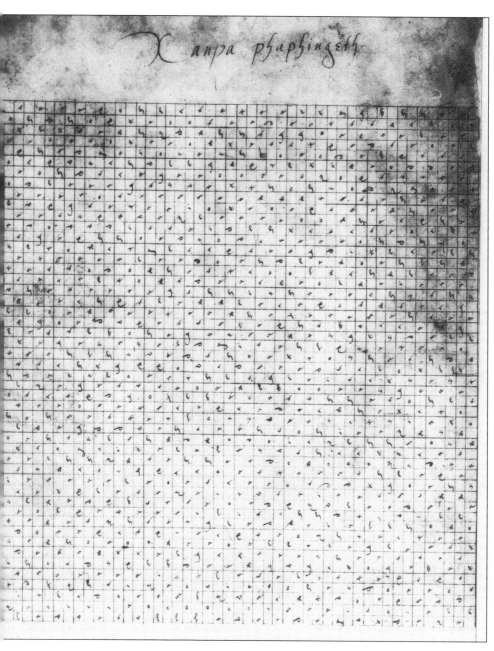

Table 36

Leaf 36 — back side

Table 37

Leaf 37 – front side

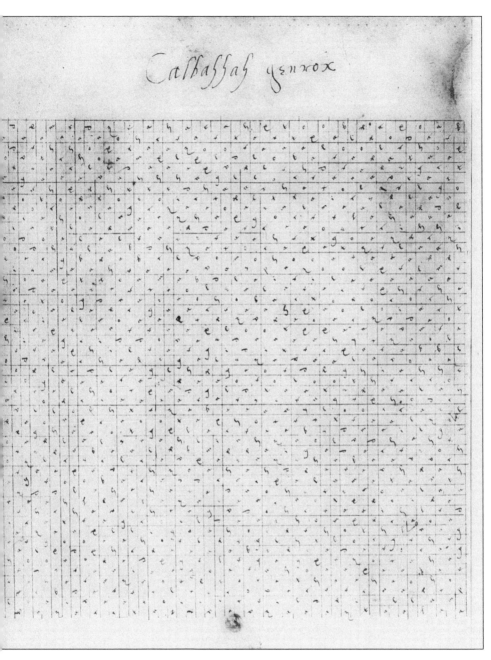

Table 37

Leaf 37 – back side

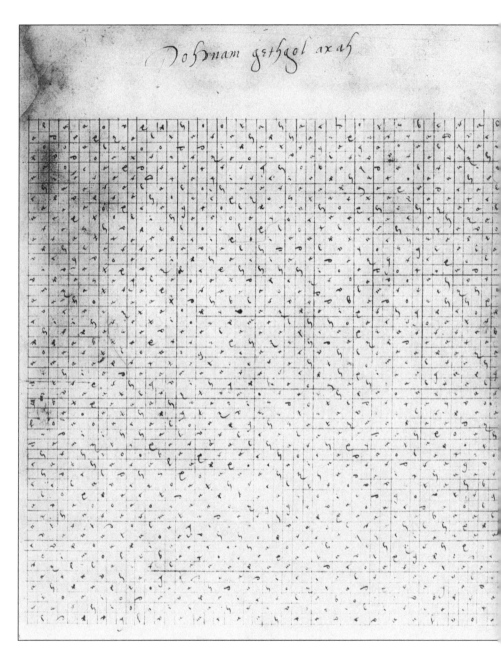

Table 38

Leaf 38 – front side

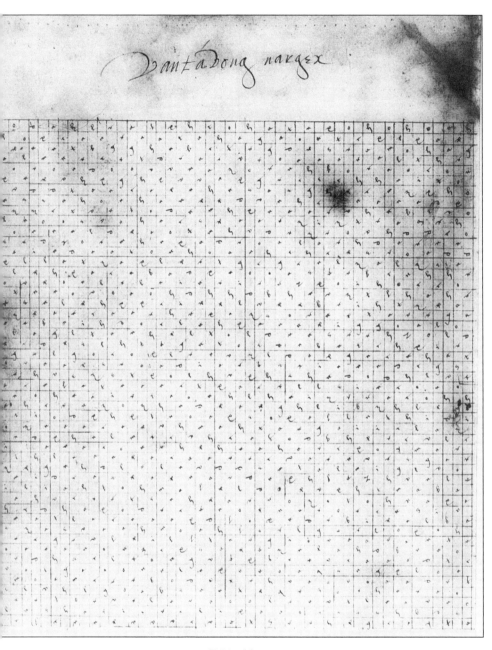

Table 38

Leaf 38 – back side

Table 39

Leaf 39 – front side

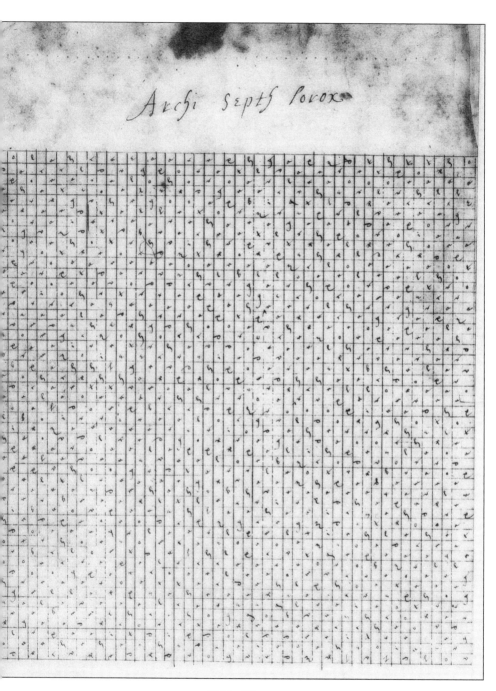

Table 39

Leaf 39 – back side

Table 40

Leaf 40 — front side

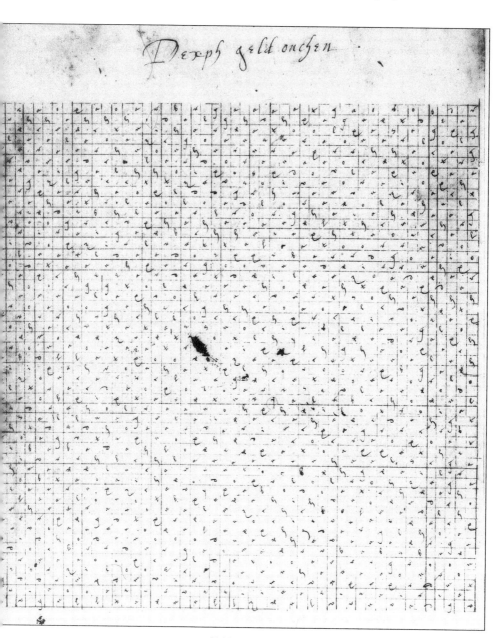

Table 40

Leaf 40 – back side

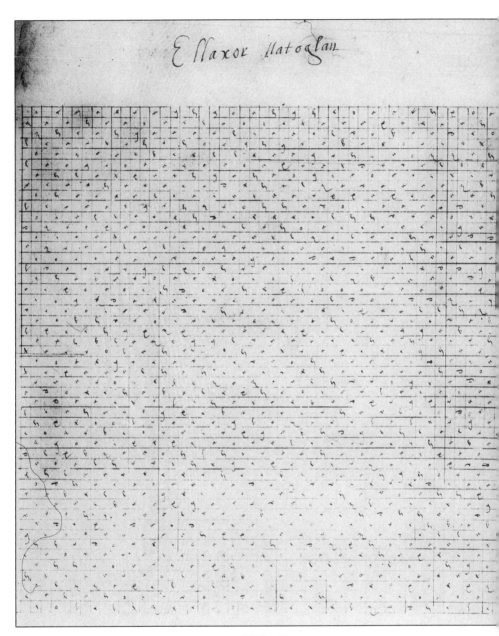

Table 41

Leaf 41 – front side

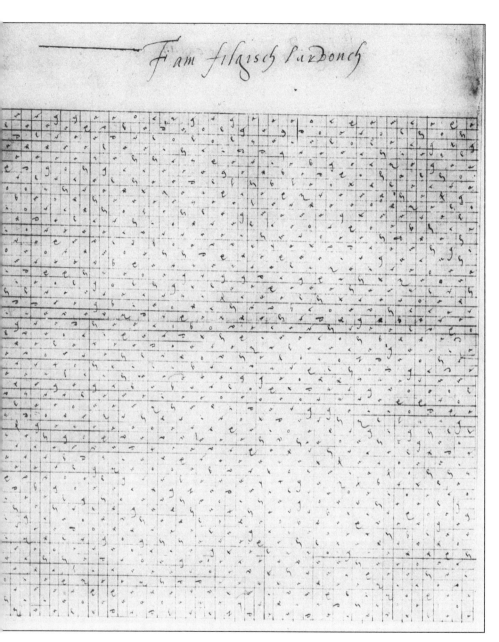

Table 41

Leaf 41 – back side

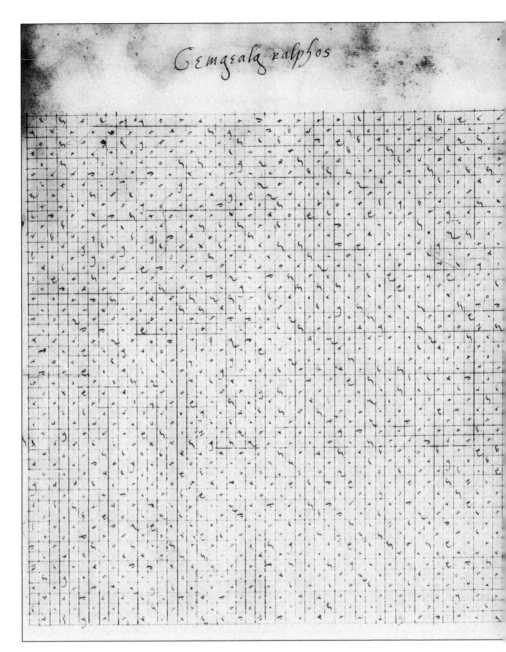

Table 42

Leaf 42 – front side

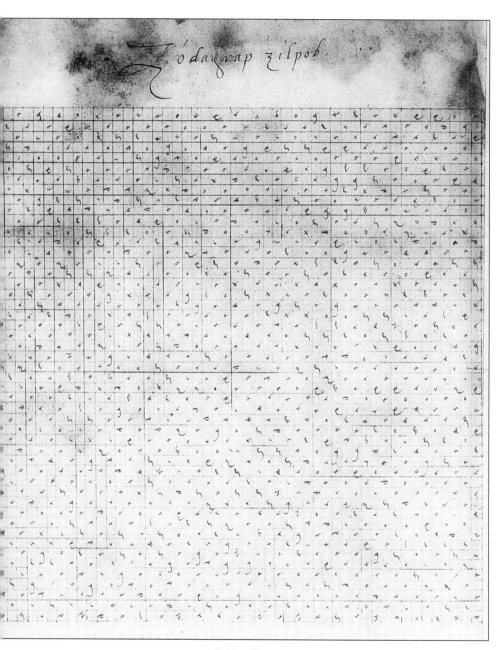

Table 42

Leaf 42 – back side

Table 43

Leaf 43 – front side

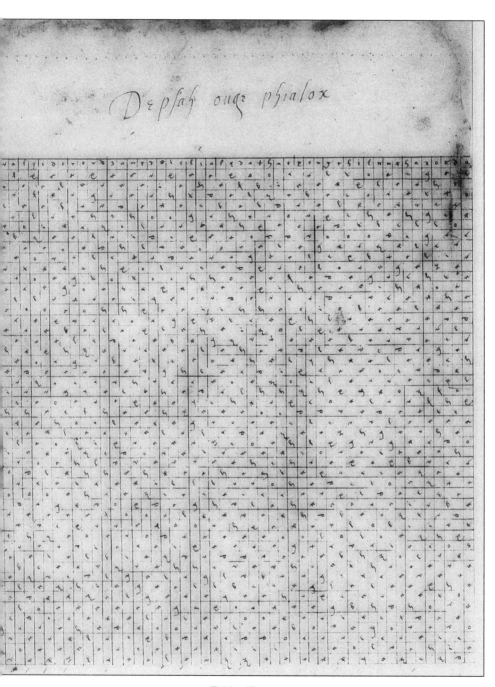

Table 43

Leaf 43 – back side

Table 44

Leaf 44 – front side

Table 44

Leaf 44 – back side

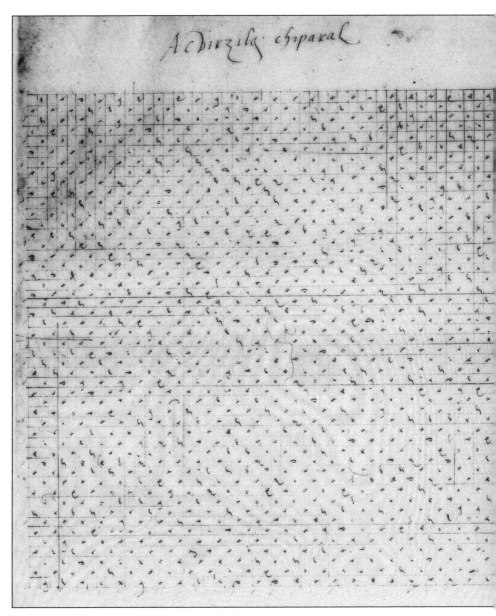

Table 45

Leaf 45 – front side

Table 45

Leaf 45 – back side

Table 46

Leaf 46 – front side

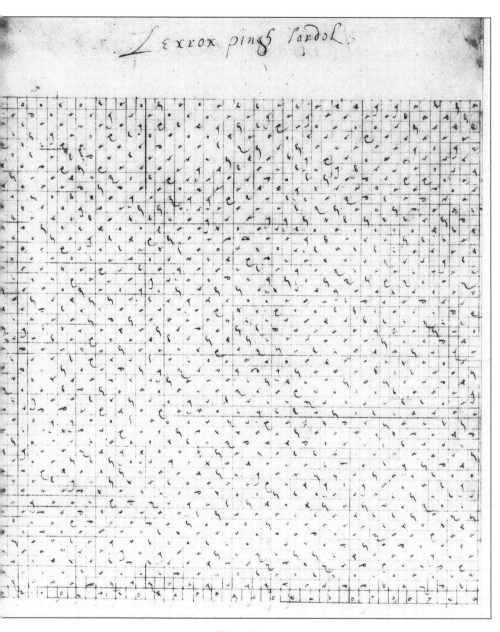

Table 46

Leaf 46 – back side

Table 47

Leaf 47 – front side

Table 47

Leaf 47 – back side

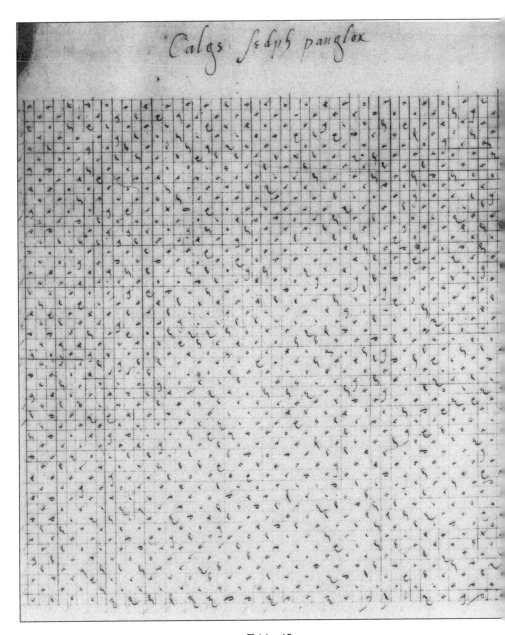

Table 48

Leaf 48 – front side

Table 48

Leaf 48 – back side

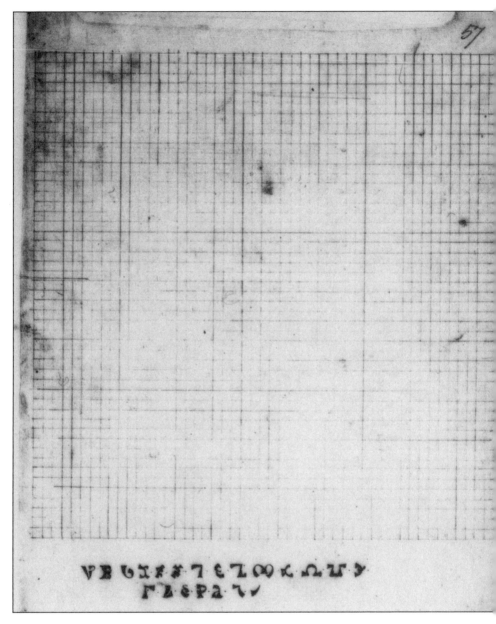

The last page of the Book of Enoch,
showing the twenty-one characters of the
Enochian alphabet as traced by Edward Kelley

NOTES

Chapter 1. Enoch of the Bible

1. *The Lost Books of the Bible,* 45.
2. Ibid., 46.
3. Ibid., 53, 54.
4. Ibid., 87.
5. Laurence, *The Book of Enoch the Prophet,* 7, 8.

Chapter 2. The Apocryphal Book of Enoch

1. Bruce, *Travels to Discover the Source of the Nile,* 422.
2. Blavatsky, *The Secret Doctrine,* Volume 2, 535.

Chapter 4. Dr. John Dee and the Angels

1. Casaubon, *A True and Faithful Relation,* 174.

Chapter 5. Dr. Dee Receives the Book of Enoch

1. Casaubon, *A True and Faithful Relation,* 3.
2. Ibid., 199.
3. Ibid., 78.
4. Ibid., 64–65.
5. Sloane 3188, f101b., manuscript from the British Library.
6. Casaubon, *A True and Faithful Relation,* 77.
7. Ibid., 209.
8. Ibid., 88.

9. Peterson, *John Dee's Five Books of Mystery,* 263.

10. Ibid., 393–94.

11. Ibid., 351.

12. Casaubon, *A True and Faithful Relation,* 199.

13. Sloane 3188 and Peterson, *John Dee's Five Books of Mystery,* 263.

Chapter 6. The Discovery of the Hidden Forty-ninth Table of the Book of Enoch

1. Casaubon, *A True and Faithful Relation,* 19.

2. Ibid., 19.

3. Ibid.

4. Ibid.

5. Ibid., 20.

6. Ibid.

7. Ibid.

8. Ibid., 21.

9. Ibid.

Chapter 9. Instructions for Meditating Using the Book of Enoch

1. Casaubon, *A True and Faithful Relation,* 77.

Chapter 10. Reflections and Final Thoughts

1. Casaubon, *A True and Faithful Relation,* 198.

2. Ibid., 161.

BIBLIOGRAPHY

Agrippa, Henry Cornelius. *De incertitudine et vanitate scientiarum et artium, atque excellentia verbi Dei declamation (Vanity of the arts and sciences).* Paris: 1531.

———. *De Occulta Philosophia.* Antwerp: 1531.

———. *De Occulta Philosophia Libri Tres.* Cologne: 1533.

———. *Three Books of Occult Philosophy.* London: 1651.

———. *The Fourth Book of Occult Philosophy.* London: 1655.

Barnstone, Willis, and Marvin Meyer, eds. *The Gnostic Bible.* Boston: New Seeds Books, 2006.

Bruce, James. *Travels to Discover the Source of the Nile, in Five Volumes.* London: J. Ruthven, 1790.

Blavatsky, H. P. *The Secret Doctrine,* 2 vols. London: 1888.

Budge, E. A. Wallis. *Egyptian Magic.* London: Kegan, Paul, Trench and Trübner & Co., 1901.

Casaubon, Meric. *A True and Faithful Relation of What Passed for Many Years Between Dr. John Dee and Some Spirits.* London: D. Maxwell, 1659. (Reprinted London: Askin Press, 1974.)

Charles, R. H., trans. *The Book of Enoch.* London: 1912.

Charlesworth, J. H. *The Old Testament Pseudepigrapha, Volume 1.* London: 1983.

Chronological Study Bible. Nashville, Tenn.: Thomas Nelson, 2008.

Clark, Andrew. *Aubrey's Brief Lives—Chiefly of Contemporaries Set down by John Aubrey between the Years 1669 and 1696.* London: 1898.

Cotton Appendix XLVI, Parts 1 and 2; Manuscripts from the British Library.

Crowley, Aleister. *The Vision and the Voice with Commentary and Other Papers.* York Beach, Maine: Samuel Weiser, 1998.

Deacon, Richard. *John Dee: Scientist, Geographer, Astrologer, and Secret Agent to Elizabeth I.* London: Frederick Muller, 1968.

Dee, John. *General and Rare Memorials Pertaining to the Perfect Art of Navigation.* London: 1577.

———. *A letter, containing a most briefe discourse apologeticall with a plaine demonstration, and feruent protestation, for the lawfull, sincere, very faithfull and Christian course, of the philosophicall studies and exercises, of a certaine studious gentleman: an ancient seruant to her most excellent Maiesty royall.* 1599.

———. *To the Kings most excellent Maiestie.* London: E. Short, 1604.

———. *The Hieroglyphic Monad.* London: John M. Watkins, 1947.

Debus, Allen G., ed. *John Dee, The Mathematicall Praeface to the Elements of Geometrie of Euclid of Megara (1570).* New York: Science History Publications, 1975.

DeSalvo, John. *Dead Sea Scrolls.* New York: Barnes and Noble, 2009.

DuQuette, Lon Milo. *Enochian Vision Magick.* San Francisco, Calif.: Weiser Books, 2008.

Elliott, J. D., ed. *The Apocryphal New Testament.* Oxford: Clarendon Press, 1993.

Fenton, Edward. *The Diaries of John Dee.* United Kingdom: Day Books, 1998.

French, Peter. *John Dee: The World of an Elizabethan Magus.* New York: Dorset Press, 1972.

Hislop, Alexander. *The Two Babylons.* New Jersey: Loizeaux Brothers, 1916.

The Holy Bible, English Standard Version (ESV). Wheaton, Ill.: Crossway Bibles, 2001.

James I, King of England. *Daemonologie in forme of a dialogue, diuided into three bookes.* Edinburgh: Robert Walde-graue, printer, 1597.

James, Geoffrey. *The Enochian Magick of Dr. John Dee.* St. Paul, Minn.: Llewellyn, 1994.

King, Leonard W. *Babylonian magic and sorcery: being "The prayers of the lifting of the hand," the cuneiform texts of a group of Babylonian and Assyrian incantations and magical formulae edited with transliterations, translations and full vocabulary from tablets of the Kuyunjik collections preserved in the British Museum.* London: Luzac and Co., 1896.

Laurence, Richard. *The Book of Enoch the Prophet*. London: Kegan Paul, Trench & Co., 1883.

Laycock, Donald C. *The Complete Enochian Dictionary*. San Francisco, Calif.: Weiser Books, 2001.

The Lost Books of the Bible. Cleveland, Ohio: The World Publishing Company, 1926.

Meyer, Marvin, ed. *The Nag Hammadi Scriptures*. New York: HarperSanFrancisco, 2007.

Morley, Henry. *Cornelius Agrippa: The Life of Henry Cornelius Agrippa von Nettesheim, Doctor and Knight, Commonly known as a Magician—2 volumes*. London: Chapman and Hall, 1856.

Nauert, Charles G., Jr. *Agrippa and the Crisis of Renaissance Thought*. Urbana: University of Illinois, 1965.

NIV Archaeological Study Bible. Grand Rapids, Mich.: Zondervan, 2005.

Peterson, Joseph H. *John Dee's Five Books of Mystery*. San Francisco, Calif.: Weiser Books, 2003.

Raphael. *The Familiar Astrologer*. London: T. Noble, 1849.

Regardie, Israel. *The Golden Dawn*. St. Paul, Minn.: Llewellyn, 1971.

Russell, George William (AE). *The Candle of Vision*. London: Macmillan and Co., 1918.

Russell, Walter. *The Universal One*. New York: Brieger Press, 1926.

Schneemelcher, William, ed. *The New Testament Apocrypha I*. Louisville, Ky.: Westminster John Knox Press, 1991.

Shumaker, Wayne, ed. and trans. *John Dee on Astronomy—Propaedeumata Aphoristica (1558 & 1568)*. Berkeley: University of California Press, 1978.

Skinner, Stephen, and David Rankine. *Practical Angel Magic of Dr. John Dee's Enochian Tables*. London: Golden Hoard Press, 2004.

Sloane 3188, 3189, 3191; Manuscripts from the British Library.

Smith, Charlotte Fell. *John Dee (1527–1608)*. London: Constable and Company, 1909.

Sparks, H. F. D. *The Apocryphal Old Testament*. New York: Oxford University Press, 1984.

Spence, Lewis. *An Encyclopedia of Occultism*. New York: Dodd, Mead, and Co., 1920.

Suster, Gerald. *John Dee: Essential Readings*. Great Britain: Crucible, 1986.

Turner, Robert. *The Heptarchia Mystica of John Dee*. Great Britain: The Aquarian Press, 1986.

——. *Elizabethan Magic*. Great Britain: Element Books, 1989.

Tyson, Donald. *Three Books of Occult Philosophy*. St. Paul, Minn.: Llewellyn, 1993.

——. *Enochian Magic for Beginners*. St. Paul, Minn.: Llewellyn, 2007.

Vermes, Genza. *The Complete Dead Sea Scrolls in English*. New York: Penguin Books, 1997.

Vinci, Leo. *An Enochian Dictionary GMICALZOMA*. England: Authors OnLine, 2006.

Wise, Michael, Martin Abegg Jr., and Edward Cook. *The Dead Sea Scrolls: A New Translation*. New York: HarperSanFranciso, 2005.

ABOUT THE
AUTHOR

John DeSalvo, Ph.D., is director of the Great Pyramid of Giza Research Association. His purpose in starting this association was to make available to the public general information and new research on the Great Pyramid and to post the work of pyramid researchers who may not have had the opportunity to publish their work in the traditional academic journals.

A former college professor and administrator, his B.S. degree is in physics, and his M.A. and Ph.D. degrees are in biophysics. He has taught the following subjects on the college level: human anatomy and physiology, biochemistry, general biology, human gross anatomy, and neurophysiology. His college administrative experience includes cultural affairs director, basic science department head, and dean of student affairs.

In 1979 DeSalvo coauthored the book *Human Anatomy—A Study Guide* (currently out of print) with Dr. Stanley Stolpe, former head of the Anatomy Department at the University of Illinois. His publications in scientific journals include research on the infrared system of rattlesnakes ("Spatial Properties of Primary Infrared Neurons in Crotalidae"). He was also a recipient of research grants and fellowships from the National Science Foundation, United States Public Health and Human Services, and the National Institutes of Health.

For more than twenty years, John DeSalvo was one of the scientists involved in studying the Shroud of Turin. Currently, he is executive vice president of ASSIST (Association of Scientists and Scholars International for the Shroud of Turin), which is the largest and oldest research association in the world currently studying the Shroud of Turin. He was also a research consultant to the original STURP (Shroud of Turin Research Project) team and was the contributing science editor for the book *SINDON—A Layman's Guide to the Shroud of Turin* (published in 1982, currently out of print). His Shroud research involved the image formation process of the man on the Shroud and studies using three-dimensional reconstruction, spectroscopic, and ultraviolet analysis. He has lectured nationwide on the Shroud, and in 1980 the International Platform Association designated him as one of the top thirty speakers in the nation.

He published *The Complete Pyramid Sourcebook* in 2003 and *Andrew Jackson Davis: The First American Prophet and Clairvoyant* in 2005. His book *Decoding the Pyramids* was published by Barnes and Noble in May 2008 and has been translated into French, Spanish, Italian, Dutch, and Czech.

In October 2008, his book *The Seeress of Prevorst: Her Secret Language and Prophecies from the Spirit World* was published by Inner Traditions. His book *Dead Sea Scrolls* was published by Barnes and Noble in July 2009 and is also available in French, Dutch, Spanish, and German.

His most recent book, *The Lost Art of Enochian Magic,* was published by Destiny Books in 2010 and features a CD of DeSalvo pronouncing the Enochian Calls.

ACKNOWLEDGMENTS

I'm immeasurably indebted to my very close friends Marty and Judy Stuart for their constant help and encouragement and especially to Judy for reading the entire manuscript and making invaluable suggestions.

Joseph Peterson explained to me the organization and makeup of the Tables in the Book of Enoch, especially the first leaf. I'm also very grateful to him for permission to quote from his most excellent and valuable book, *John Dee's Five Books of Mystery.*

There are very few people in the world that one is eternally grateful to, but Jon Graham is one of those people in my life. He is responsible for seeing that my most important spiritual books are published.

To my editor Anne Dillion. This is the third book Anne has assisted me with, for which I am thankful.

A very special thanks to Jeanie Levitan, the managing editor for Inner Traditions. No managing editor could take more interest in all the books she publishes and try to make them the best they could be. Her personal editorial assistance made this historic book into something that we are all very proud of.

INDEX